# TOPIC-FOCUSED APPROACH TO THE TOEFL ITP® TEST

TOEFL, TOEFL iBT, TOEFL ITP are registered trademarks of Educational Testing Service (ETS).
This publication / product / website is not endorsed or approved by ETS.

Masaaki Ogura  Shoma Aota  Koki Sekitani
Arnold Arao  Kazuya Kito  Takeshi Sato

photographs by
iStockphoto
shutterstock

## 音声ファイルのダウンロードについて

CD マークがある箇所は、ダウンロードすることも可能です。下記 URL の書籍詳細ページにあるダウンロードアイコンをクリックしてください。

https://www.seibido.co.jp/ad720

### TOPIC-FOCUSED APPROACH TO THE TOEFL ITP® TEST
頻出トピックで攻略するTOEFL ITP® TEST

Copyright © 2025 by Masaaki Ogura, Shoma Aota, Koki Sekitani, Arnold Arao, Kazuya Kito, Takeshi Sato
All rights reserved.

*All rights reserved for Japan.*
*No part of this book may be reproduced in any form*
*without permission from Seibido Co., Ltd.*

# はじめに

本書はTOEFL ITP®テストに準拠した出題形式で，TOEFLに頻出する主要な学術的トピックを学ぶことでアカデミック英語の導入を図ることを目指したテキストです．将来的なiBT受験も見据えて作成しています．TOEFLの傾向を入念に分析したうえで，全てのユニットを実際のテストと同じListening Comprehension, Structure and Written Expression, Reading Comprehensionの3つのセクションで構成し，トピックもTOEFLを意識して選定しました．また，著者陣は大学等でのTOEFL ITPの教授経験が豊富なメンバーによって構成されており，大学生がTOEFLの形式でアカデミック英語を学ぶうえでの指導のポイントを押さえた解説や活動案が取り入れられています．日本のTOEFL受験者の多くがスコアを落としやすいSection 2 (Structure and Written Expression) に関しては，質量ともに十分な演習ができるよう紙幅が割かれています．

本書の主な特徴の一つであるトピックは，一つのユニット内で様々な角度から取り上げられており，各ユニット内でその「トピック」に関する様々な基礎知識を身に付けられるよう工夫されています．また，日本の大学生がより身近で取り組みやすさを感じられるよう，そのトピックに関する定番の難しい話題ばかりではなく，より最近の話題を取り入れていることもポイントの一つです．問題演習を行うことでそれぞれの学術的トピックについて興味を持てば，さらなる自律的学習につながっていくでしょうし，様々なトピックに関する基礎的知識を身に付けることは，大学での学びを支える教養に触れることでもあります．

本来TOEFLは北米の大学に入学するために必要な英語力を測ることが目的のテストであるため，日本の英語学習者にとっては特に語彙が難しいことで問題に取り組みにくくなる傾向が見られます．それを踏まえ本書は，すべてのユニットのすべてのセクションにおいて，そのセクションに出てくる語彙の理解を確認するためのWarm upを配置し，さらに末尾にVocabulary Exercisesとして単語の意味をより深く理解するためのタスクを設けています．さらにテキストに準拠したオンライン学習システムLinguaportaが附属されており，テキストで学んだ語彙等を授業外の好きな時間，好きな場所で学ぶことができるようになっています．語彙が増えれば理解できることも増え，TOEFLに対して少しずつ自信を深められるはずです．

本書は将来TOEFLを受験する人のための対策として，これから国内外の大学に入学する人たちの準備として，そして大学で専門的知識を学ぶ上でのベースとなるアカデミック英語の入門書として，授業内でも授業外でも学習に取り組みやすい内容と形式を備えています．本書がアカデミックなトピックを学ぶ楽しさと喜びを得るための一助となることを願ってやみません．分かる，理解できる喜びをぜひ一緒に体感しましょう！

2024年10月
著者一同

# 本書の使い方

　各ユニットではTOEFL ITP®テストと同じ順番でセクションが構成されています。ユニットごとに区切りながら模擬試験形式で問題演習を行うことが可能です。まずそれぞれのセクションの最初にある解き方のポイントを読み，Warm upで単語のチェックを行った上で問題演習を行い，出てきた語彙の定着を図るためのVocabulary Exercisesを備えています。

　各ユニットではどのセクションも1つのトピックを扱っていますので，問題を解く前後にそのトピックの背景知識について教員からの説明を聞いたり，他の学習者と意見を交換したりするタスクを行ってもよいでしょう。TOEFLに頻出するトピックに幅広く触れるために，できるだけ偏りなく全てのユニットに触れることをおすすめします。

　各セクションは以下のように構成されています。

## Section 1 (Listening Comprehension)

Part A, Part B, Part Cの3つの問題形式のうち，各Unitにはそのうちの2つを配置しています。互いに独立しているため，どちらか一方のみを取り扱うことも可能です。

## Section 2 (Structure and Written Expression)

Structure Exercisesを7問，Written Expressionsを7問配置しています。重要な内容が身につくよう，意図的に似たような問題が繰り返し出てくるように工夫しています。

## Section 3 (Reading Comprehension)

本試験とほぼ同じ約350語のパッセージに，設問を8問付しています。最初は少し時間をかけて解いてもよいですが，徐々に本試験の時間（10-11分）に近づけるとよいでしょう。

　授業外では，出版社ホームページからリスニング用音源をダウンロードし，音声にあわせて音読やディクテーション，シャドーイングが実施できます。またLinguaportaを用いて復習を行うと，授業の内容がより定着するでしょう。

執筆担当
Section 1：青田 庄真，小倉 雅明
Section 2：小倉 雅明
Section 3：佐藤 健，関谷 弘毅
各Sectionの解説文及び全体の助言：鬼頭 和也
英文校閲：Arnold Arao

# CONTENTS

**UNIT 1** ......................................... 1
## History (1)

**UNIT 2** ......................................... 9
## Psychology (1)

**UNIT 3** ......................................... 17
## Environment (1)

**UNIT 4** ......................................... 25
## Science and Technology (1)

**UNIT 5** ......................................... 33
## Biology (1)

**UNIT 6** ......................................... 41
## Art (1)

**UNIT 7** ......................................... 49
## Economics (1)

**UNIT 8** ......................................... 57
## History (2)

**UNIT 9** ......................................... 65
## Psychology (2)

**UNIT 10** ......................................... 73
## Environment (2)

**UNIT 11** ......................................... 81
## Science and Technology (2)

**UNIT 12** ......................................... 89
## Biology (2)

**UNIT 13** ......................................... 97
## Art (2)

**UNIT 14** ......................................... 105
## Economics (2)

## リンガポルタのご案内

> リンガポルタ連動テキストをご購入の学生さんは、
> 「リンガポルタ」を無料でご利用いただけます！

　本テキストで学習していただく内容に準拠した問題を、オンライン学習システム「リンガポルタ」で学習していただくことができます。PCだけでなく、スマートフォンやタブレットでも学習できます。単語や文法、リスニング力などをよりしっかり身に付けていただくため、ぜひ積極的に活用してください。

　リンガポルタの利用にはアカウントとアクセスコードの登録が必要です。登録方法については下記ページにアクセスしてください。

### https://www.seibido.co.jp/linguaporta/register.html

本テキスト「TOPIC-FOCUSED APPROACH TO THE TOEFL ITP® TEST」のアクセスコードは下記です。

### 7315-2049-1231-0365-0003-008a-QV75-S9QP

・リンガポルタの学習機能（画像はサンプルです。また、すべてのテキストに以下の4つの機能が用意されているわけではありません）

●多肢選択

●空所補充（音声を使っての聞き取り問題も可能）

●単語並びかえ（マウスや手で単語を移動）

●マッチング（マウスや手で単語を移動）

# UNIT 1

# History (1)

## 1. Listening Comprehension

Listening Section は 3 つのパートで構成されます．Part A では短い会話，Part B ではやや長めの会話，Part C では長めのスピーチを聞いて設問に答えます．いずれの Part も設問が印刷されていないので，その部分まで音声を聞き取る必要があります．Part A は短いですが，答えが直接的に言及されていない場合が多いため注意が必要です．次の行動を類推させる形式や発話の意図を尋ねる形式など，まずは典型的なパターンに慣れていきましょう．

### Warm up

英語に対応する日本語を選びましょう．

1. archaeological    (　)    a. やりがいのある
2. multiple          (　)    b. 考古学上の
3. confirm           (　)    c. 複数の
4. challenging       (　)    d. 確認する

### Listening Exercises (1)  1-02〜04

Part A と同じ形式の問題を解きましょう．この Part は，短い会話とそれに続く 1 つの質問から成ります．質問に対する最も適切な解答をそれぞれ (A)–(D) から選びましょう．

1. (A) She recently moved to the home.
   (B) She dislikes dry climates.
   (C) She specializes in insect ecology.
   (D) She and the man live in the same neighborhood.

2. (A) He is already a member of that professor's seminar.
   (B) He does not want to join that professor's seminar.
   (C) He does not find assignments to be a burden at all.
   (D) He is trying to take the same class as the woman.

3. (A) Check notices that have been posted for students
   (B) Look for a friend who is taking the same class
   (C) Visit the instructor's office
   (D) Move to the classroom where the class is held

## Listening Exercises (2)    CD 1-05, 06

Part C と同じ形式の問題を解きましょう．この Part は，長めの講義・スピーチとそれに続く複数の質問から成ります．質問に対する最も適切な解答をそれぞれ (A)–(D) から選びましょう．

1. (A) Class rules that students should follow
   (B) An international exhibition on the latest technology
   (C) Difficulties involved in archaeological research
   (D) Procedure for participation in the quiz competition

2. (A) Technology such as drones for 3D scanning is developing.
   (B) The number of researchers interested in archaeology is increasing.
   (C) The Egyptian government has invested heavily in research.
   (D) The popularity of museums is growing.

3. (A) 8 %
   (B) 15 %
   (C) 30 %
   (D) 70 %

4. (A) Go to a museum with the students
   (B) Explain the outline of the class content
   (C) Continue explaining class policies
   (D) Check attendance for this class

## Vocabulary Building (Section 1)

このセクションに登場した単語を辞書で調べ，意味を書きましょう．また，調べた単語を使って，英文を完成させましょう．

(A) attendance   (n) _____     (D) policy     (n) _____
(B) exclude      (v) _____     (E) overview   (n) _____
(C) in advance   (adv) _____   (F) outline    (v) _____

1. The professor asked us to _____ the problem using the diagram on the whiteboard.
2. The best _____ would be for them to refuse to comment on such matters.
3. This spreadsheet gives us a(n) _____ of the competition results.

UNIT 1 History (1)

## 2. Structure and Written Expression

Structure and Written Expression は，TOEFL ITP では文法・語法問題に相当します．Structure は文中の空欄に適切な語句を補充する問題，Written Expression は文を読んで文法・語法的な誤りの箇所を指摘する問題です．トピックに固有の難しい語彙は登場しますが，問われている項目は基本的な内容であることも少なくありません．最終的に時間をかけずに解いていくことが求められますが，まずは時間をかけて解いてみましょう．

### Warm up

英語に対応する日本語を選びましょう．

1. abundant ( )     a. 拡大
2. structural ( )     b. 豊富な
3. expansion ( )     c. 構造上の
4. primary ( )     d. 主要な

### Structure Exercises

空欄に入る最も適切な語句を (A)–(D) から選び，英文を完成させましょう．

1. While it is often mentioned that the Roman Empire faced structural _____, there are researchers who remain skeptical about this point.

   (A) milestones
   (B) achievements
   (C) dilemmas
   (D) crises

2. The era of peace and stability in Rome, commonly referred to as Pax Romana, impressively spanned a _____ period of about 200 years.

   (A) lengthy
   (B) concise
   (C) emergent
   (D) interval

3. The decline of the Roman Empire cannot be _____ pinpointed to one specific cause.

   (A) simpler
   (B) simply
   (C) simplest
   (D) simple

4. Contrary to the widespread perception of them _____ the most formidable force, the Roman army, in reality, faced several defeats in various wars throughout its history.

   (A) was
   (B) were
   (C) being
   (D) to be

3

**5.** Within the ranks of the Roman army, it was primarily the privileged nobles, those _____ both high status and abundant wealth, who were given the esteemed role of becoming cavalry.

(A) had
(B) have had
(C) having
(D) have

**6.** As the Roman Empire transitioned into its imperial era, with the political landscape _____ a remarkable stabilization, wars aiming at territorial expansion, along with internal civil unrest, saw a significant decline.

(A) was experienced
(B) experiencing
(C) experienced
(D) experience

**7.** In the year 313, Emperor Constantine made a bold move for the sake of internal stability; he officially _____ Christianity, which was a remarkable shift in the empire's religious climate.

(A) finalized
(B) pointed
(C) mediated
(D) recognized

## Written Expression Exercises

英文中の誤った箇所を (A)–(D) から選びましょう.

**1.** Theodosius, who holds the distinction of being the lastly sole emperor of the Roman
    A                                    B
Empire, took the significant step of declaring Christianity as the official state religion.
                                        C                    D

**2.** Among the leading cause behind the fall of the Roman Empire, the weakening economic
     A            B                                              C
strength stands out, a decline that was notably exemplified by the evident deterioration of
                    D
their infrastructure.

**3.** Unlike to the abrupt fall of civilizations like Carthage, the Roman Empire's decline was
     A                                        B
a more gradual process, unfolding over a longer stretch of time.
   C                    D

**4.** Carthage faced a tragic fate of it was completely and mercilessly destroyed by Rome in
                            A                                        B
the series of devastating confrontations known as the Punic Wars.
   C                                    D

4

UNIT 1 History (1)

5. Among the myriad reasons for the decline of the Roman Empire, the primary factors
   **A**                                                              **B**
   were internal divisions coupled with the constant threat of invasions from neighbored
                           **C**                                              **D**
   nations.

6. Just as in many ancient civilizations, in Rome too, a stable security environment paved
   **A**
   the way for thriving trade routes and active exchanges of goods, which lead to a period
                **B**                                                      **C**
   of commercial prosperity.
      **D**

7. During the times when the Roman Empire dominating Europe, the continent was
                    **A**                       **B**
   significantly influenced by its culture and legal systems, which spread far and wide.
   **C**                                                       **D**

## Vocabulary Building (Section 2)

> このセクションに登場した単語を辞書で調べ，意味を書きましょう．また，調べた単語を使って，
> 英文を完成させましょう．

(A) milestone   (n) _____     (D) formidable   (adj) _____
(B) stability   (n) _____     (E) privileged   (adj) _____
(C) specific    (adj) _____   (F) unrest       (n) _____

1. Financial _____ is essential for a secure and prosperous future.
2. The city is very quiet today despite the _____.
3. The _____ opponent dominated the game, leaving the other team with no chance to
   win.

## 3. Reading Comprehension

Reading では，350 語程度のパッセージを 5 つ読んで，それぞれ内容に関する設問を解くことが求められます．様々なトピックについての英文が出題されるため一見難しく感じるかもしれませんが，トピックの背景知識がないと解けないような問題はありません．本番では読む時間を含めて 1 問 1 分で解く必要がありますが，最初は焦らず問題に取り組みましょう．

### Warm up

英語に対応する日本語を選びましょう．

| | | | |
|---|---|---|---|
| 1. ancient | ( ) | a. | 清涼飲料水 |
| 2. magnitude | ( ) | b. | ぐつぐつ煮る |
| 3. ritual | ( ) | c. | 儀式 |
| 4. simmer | ( ) | d. | 古代の |
| 5. refreshment | ( ) | e. | 大きさ |

### Reading Exercises

次の文章を読み，下の問いに対する最も適切な解答をそれぞれ (A)–(D) から選びましょう．

A remarkable discovery was made in the city of Giza, Egypt. Scientists believe they have uncovered the oldest brewery in the world within an ancient tomb. This extraordinary revelation provides a unique perspective on the ancient Egyptian way of life and culture. The magnitude of the ruins indicates that the production of lager, a type of beer brewed and
5 conditioned at low temperature, was a significant endeavor. At any given moment, the brewery was capable of producing thousands of liters of beer. According to authorities, this beer was utilized not only for everyday consumption but also for ceremonial intents.

During ancient times, alcohol served a purpose beyond mere enjoyment. It was indispensable to a great number of religious rituals and ceremonies. It is possible that this
10 brewery's beer was utilized in religious observances, feasts, and offerings to the gods. The site's instruments and tools are straightforward yet highly efficient. Utilizing a sizable ceramic receptacle, the ingredients were combined, and the beer was fermented. Additionally, there was a location to simmer and filter the beer. This configuration and design demonstrate that the ancient Egyptians had a solid knowledge of the brewing process.

15 This finding is significant because it alters our understanding of ancient Egyptian society. It demonstrates that in addition to architecture and art, they possessed sophisticated knowledge and abilities in brewing. The brewery's estimated age of existence exceeds five thousand five hundred years. This suggests that it was built in conjunction with the construction of the Pyramids of Giza. Pyramid builders might have been granted beer either
20 as a form of compensation or as a refreshment.

This finding has garnered international recognition. This ancient brewery has been frequented by numerous tourists and experts who are anxious to learn more. This finding adds

6

to the long list of wonders Egypt is proud of. The discovery of this historic brewery shed light on the importance that ancient Egyptians placed on alcohol. Additionally, it reveals their remarkable knowledge and skill. The rich history and treasures of Egypt continue to captivate 25 and astonish us.

1. What is the main idea of the passage?
   (A) The architectural wonders of ancient Egypt
   (B) The discovery and significance of an ancient brewery in Giza
   (C) The daily life and habits of ancient Egyptians
   (D) The trading systems of ancient Egypt

2. The word "brewery" in line 2 is closest in meaning to
   (A) winery
   (B) distillery
   (C) pub
   (D) beer factory

3. What did the ruins suggest about lager production?
   (A) It was a major effort.
   (B) It was primarily for export.
   (C) It was a small-scale activity.
   (D) It was outsourced to neighboring cities.

4. For what purposes was the beer likely used during ancient times?
   (A) Solely for everyday consumption
   (B) Mainly for medicinal purposes
   (C) For ceremonial intents and daily consumption
   (D) Exclusively for the royal family

5. The word "it" in line 15 refers to
   (A) the fact that beer was used in religious rituals
   (B) the tools and instruments at the site
   (C) the city of Giza
   (D) the discovery of the ancient brewery

6. What relation does the brewery's formation have with the Pyramids of Giza?
   (A) Its formation took place in conjunction with the pyramids.
   (B) The brewery was constructed long after the pyramids.
   (C) They were constructed by different civilizations.
   (D) The brewery was a blueprint for the pyramids.

**7.** How has the discovery of the brewery been received internationally?

(A) It has earned praise from around the world.

(B) It sparked controversies and debates.

(C) It was ignored by the global community.

(D) Questions were raised about its authenticity.

**8.** According to the passage, which statement is NOT true?

(A) The ancient Egyptians used beer primarily for casual enjoyment.

(B) The tools at the site were simple but effective.

(C) The brewery is believed to be older than five thousand years.

(D) The brewery's discovery has attracted many tourists and experts.

## Vocabulary Building (Section 3)

このセクションに登場した単語を辞書で調べ，意味を書きましょう．また，調べた単語を使って，英文を完成させましょう．

| | | | |
|---|---|---|---|
| (A) endeavor | (n) _____ | (D) straightforward (adj) _____ | |
| (B) utilize | (v) _____ | (E) alter (v) _____ | |
| (C) consumption | (n) _____ | (F) sophisticated (adj) _____ | |

**1.** Excessive _____ of junk food can lead to health problems.

**2.** It's important to _____ modern technology effectively in today's business world.

**3.** The system they designed was highly _____ and advanced.

8

# UNIT 2
# Psychology (1)

## 1. Listening Comprehension

Part C の問題形式は，Listening Section では唯一モノローグ形式になっています．基本的には，あるトピックに関する専門家による講義の一部などが素材となっています．したがって，様々な学問分野における頻出トピックやそれに関連する語彙について，事前知識を持っていることが重要となります．例えば本章で取り上げる心理学の中でも，生理心理学，認知心理学，発達心理学，心理統計学など，どのような話題があり得るのか把握に努めましょう．

 **Warm up**

英語に対応する日本語を選びましょう．

1. reliable         (　　)    a. 意識的な，意識している
2. psychological    (　　)    b. 考え出す，解決する
3. conscious        (　　)    c. 信頼できる，信頼性のある
4. figure out       (　　)    d. 心理（学）の

 **Listening Exercises (1)**  1-07, 08

Part B と同じ形式の問題を解きましょう．この Part は，長めの会話とそれに続く複数の質問から成ります．質問に対する最も適切な解答をそれぞれ (A)–(D) から選びましょう．

1. (A) Yesterday's handball match
   (B) Homework assigned to them
   (C) The selection of books in the library
   (D) Types of bulletin boards they have to pay attention to

2. (A) Because he was nervous about the handball game.
   (B) Because he was looking for a paper written by Professor Neuse.
   (C) Because he had to prepare an experiment in the laboratory.
   (D) Because he was reading an article written by Professor Murton.

3. (A) He is the coach of a handball club.
   (B) He was a professor of statistics at the college until last year.
   (C) He is the professor who gave the report.
   (D) He is a psychological counselor at the school.

9

## Listening Exercises (2)  🎧 1-09, 10

Part C と同じ形式の問題を解きましょう．この Part は，長めの講義・スピーチとそれに続く複数の質問から成ります．質問に対する最も適切な解答をそれぞれ (A)–(D) から選びましょう．

**1.** (A) How to communicate better
   (B) How to speak effectively in court
   (C) How to detect lies
   (D) How to form a better relationship with people through lies

**2.** (A) People believe lying will give them a big advantage in conversations.
   (B) People hope that things they lie about will come true someday.
   (C) People want to escape from awkward situations.
   (D) People want to create a better image of themselves.

**3.** (A) Our cognitive function is completely out of our conscious control.
   (B) A large proportion of our cognitive function is controllable.
   (C) Only a small proportion or our cognitive function can be consciously controlled.
   (D) Half of our cognitive function can be controlled while the other half cannot.

**4.** (A) A strong disbelief in yourself
   (B) Selfish behavior toward other people
   (C) A modified attitude toward people who are close to you
   (D) Using speech differently

## Vocabulary Building (Section 1)

このセクションに登場した単語を辞書で調べ，意味を書きましょう．また，調べた単語を使って，英文を完成させましょう．

| | | | | |
|---|---|---|---|---|
| (A) detect | (v) _____ | (D) fantasy | (n) _____ | |
| (B) literature | (n) _____ | (E) monitor | (v) _____ | |
| (C) circumstance | (n) _____ | (F) torture | (n) _____ | |

**1.** His stories seemed like a _____, so no one is convinced now.
**2.** Surprisingly, there is not much _____ on this subject.
**3.** This machine can _____ alcohol on your breath.

UNIT 2 Psychology (1)

# 2. Structure and Written Expression

TOEFL ITP の Section 2 では，基本的な英文法の理解が得点アップの鍵となります．時制，主語と動詞の一致，冠詞や前置詞の正しい使い方など，まずは重要な文法事項をしっかりと学習しましょう．基本事項が確実に理解できていれば，複雑な問題にも対応できるようになってきます．また，学習した内容を自分の言葉で説明できるようにすると，理解がさらに深まります．

## Warm up

英語に対応する日本語を選びましょう．

1. perspective     (　)     **a.** 分類
2. classification     (　)     **b.** 知覚
3. cognition     (　)     **c.** 認知，認識
4. perception     (　)     **d.** 観点，見方

## Structure Exercises

空欄に入る最も適切な語句を (A)–(D) から選び，英文を完成させましょう．

1. During the 19th and 20th centuries, developmental psychology was heavily influenced by the study of child psychology, and this relationship was of _____.

    (A) concern
    (B) concerned
    (C) concerning
    (D) to concern

2. The problem known as identity crisis is observed at various stages of life and this problem has been studied from different _____.

    (A) perspectives
    (B) horizons
    (C) kinds
    (D) principals

3. Although emotions can be broadly categorized into positive and negative, they present a(n) _____ level of complexity and resist a binary classification.

    (A) uniform
    (B) abundant
    (C) profound
    (D) moderate

4. _____ Jean Piaget was a renowned psychologist, he initially had a keen interest in the study of animals, a field known as zoology.

    (A) Whereas
    (B) In spite of
    (C) Conversely
    (D) However

11

5. Motivation has been studied in the field of psychology, _____ it has also been analyzed from a philosophical point of view.

(A) what's more
(B) in the meantime
(C) in contrast
(D) and

6. It would be premature to assume that smartphones are the direct _____ of memory loss; in fact, there are many factors involved.

(A) cause
(B) because
(C) result
(D) way

7. The connotation of the term "learning" in everyday usage does not necessarily _____ with its application in psychological contexts.

(A) react
(B) depend
(C) respond
(D) correspond

## Written Expression Exercises

英文中の誤った箇所を (A)–(D) から選びましょう.

1. Cognitive dissonance refers to the discomfort of people have when they find
   **A**              **B**          **C**
   discrepancies between the cognitions they have and other information.
   **D**

2. Some theories hold that humans are born with the need to forming an emotional bond
   **A**                          **B**
   with their caregivers, and that this bond develops within the first six months under
   **C**                               **D**
   caregivers' appropriate response.

3. Narcissism is characterized by extreme self-importance and a desire for admiration from
   **A**                                                    **B**
   others, according to Freud is a normal stage of child development.
   **C**                                       **D**

4. Among the goal of Gestalt psychology in the 20th century was to identify the brain
   **A**                          **B**
   functions behind the mechanisms of perception.
   **C**          **D**

**5.** One of the studies $\underset{\text{A}}{\underline{\text{on}}}$ forgetting $\underset{\text{B}}{\underline{\text{aims}}}$ to clarify what $\underset{\text{C}}{\underline{\text{elements related}}}$ to in the $\underset{\text{D}}{\underline{\text{forgetting}}}$ rate.

**6.** Not $\underset{\text{A}}{\underline{\text{every}}}$ behaviors can be acquired $\underset{\text{B}}{\underline{\text{through}}}$ learning, and there are innate $\underset{\text{C}}{\underline{\text{factors}}}$ $\underset{\text{D}}{\underline{\text{involved}}}$.

**7.** The concept $\underset{\text{A}}{\underline{\text{of}}}$ behavior therapy $\underset{\text{B}}{\underline{\text{originating}}}$ from $\underset{\text{C}}{\underline{\text{studies}}}$ by $\underset{\text{D}}{\underline{\text{Russian psychologist}}}$ Ivan Pavlov.

## ✎ *Vocabulary Building* (Section 2)

> このセクションに登場した単語を辞書で調べ, 意味を書きましょう. また, 調べた単語を使って, 英文を完成させましょう.

(A) concerned (adj) _____ (D) correspond (v) _____

(B) acquire (v) _____ (E) cognitive (adj) _____

(C) philosophical (adj) _____ (F) identify (v) _____

**1.** The researcher is _____ with social inequality.

**2.** It should be now possible to _____ some of the causes of that behavior.

**3.** Some people believe that wealth _____s with happiness.

13

# 3. Reading Comprehension

Reading Section でも，Listening Section 同様，トピックに関する語彙の知識が重要になります．リーディングの問題は，本文を読まないと答えられないものだけでなく，語彙の知識があれば答えられるものもあります．まずは設問を眺め，どんな内容に注目して読んでいけばいいか確認してみましょう．

## Warm up

英語に対応する日本語を選びましょう．

1. determine （　） **a.** 管
2. alertness （　） **b.** 決定する
3. mercury （　） **c.** 消化
4. digestion （　） **d.** 水銀
5. vessel （　） **e.** 注意深さ

## Reading Exercises

次の文章を読み，下の問いに対する最も適切な解答をそれぞれ (A)–(D) から選びましょう．

It is often believed that your diet determines who you are. Additionally, it has been demonstrated that what you eat might enhance your emotional and mental health. A number of the items that patients eat appear to have an impact on their mental health, according to mental health experts who have been treating trauma and depression patients for years. They
5　discovered that patients' pain and depressive symptoms are reduced when they consume dark chocolate, sweet potatoes, eggs, and cherries.

Experts compare the human body to a car, and just as a car engine needs the proper type of gasoline, a person too requires the proper proportion of protein, carbohydrates, and fats. The importance of a diet high in fat is emphasized, among other things. This is because
10　the fat that makes up the brain aids in alertness, attention, and mood. The advantages of Omega-3 fatty acids for health have been the subject of extensive investigation. This fatty acid is primarily found in fish oil. However, it is also present in vegetable oils and foods like walnuts. According to experts, they may lessen grief and anxiety as well as prevent suicide. But mercury is also present in all fish. Even tiny levels of mercury can have an impact on how
15　the brain develops. Low quantities of mercury can be found in wild Pacific salmon, prawns, farmed catfish, haddock, sardines, anchovies, and other tiny fish.

However, consuming healthy fats alone is not sufficient; you also need to consume a diet that breaks down fats. For instance, it is advisable to consume dark green vegetables. Fats must be broken down by the liver and gallbladder, and green and yellow vegetables, especially
20　bitter ones, help digest fats and carry them through blood vessels to the brain, which needs them. Eating vegetables of all colors is also recommended by a lot of health professionals. Vegetables that are orange or yellow, for instance, are rich in vitamin A and have a variety of

14

UNIT 2 | Psychology (1)

other vital nutrients. Vegetables that are green or yellow are helpful for digestion. Aubergines and berries are two purple and red foods that have anti-inflammatory qualities.

Finally, according to experts, it's crucial to take the time to appreciate your meal in addition to eating correctly. In addition to eating healthily, doctors advise taking the time to enjoy your meals because doing so is good for your mental health.

1. What is the main idea of this passage?
   (A) A combination of healthy and fatty foods is important for your health.
   (B) Eating a lot of fish has a negative impact on your health due to mercury they contain.
   (C) Eating slowly and enjoyably with your family can make you feel much better.
   (D) The health of the body as well as the mind depends mainly on the foods you eat.

2. The word "they" in line 13 refers to
   (A) Omega-3 fatty acids
   (B) foods including fats
   (C) synapses
   (D) experts

3. Which food can help prevent suicide?
   (A) haddock
   (B) orange
   (C) sweet chocolate
   (D) tomato

4. Why does the author say "However, consuming healthy fats alone is not sufficient" in line 17?
   (A) Adding fatty foods to healthy foods is important.
   (B) Eating foods with less mercury can support your brain.
   (C) Eating foods that deliver fat into the blood is important.
   (D) Eating what you want to eat can support your brain.

5. The word "vital" in line 23 is closest in meaning to
   (A) adverse
   (B) imperative
   (C) hazardous
   (D) vigorous

6. The word "inflammatory" in line 24 is closest in meaning to
   (A) gratifying
   (B) sanitary
   (C) irritated
   (D) vulnerable

**7.** Which is NOT the reason why taking Omega-3 fatty acids is important?

(A) They can enhance concentration and alertness.

(B) They can help to prevent suicide.

(C) They can help to send nutrients to the brain

(D) They can lower anxiety levels.

**8.** According to the passage, which statement is NOT true?

(A) Eating fish low in mercury is recommended to take in Omega-3 fatty acids.

(B) In addition to good quality fatty acids, we need to consume foods that break them down.

(C) Professional nutritionists have suggested that certain foods boost people's moods.

(D) Spending time to enjoy meals is claimed to be important.

## Vocabulary Building (Section 3)

このセクションに登場した単語を辞書で調べ, 意味を書きましょう. また, 調べた単語を使って, 英文を完成させましょう.

(A) depression (n) ＿＿＿＿＿＿＿     (E) prevent (v) ＿＿＿＿＿＿＿

(B) proper (adj) ＿＿＿＿＿＿＿     (F) digest (v) ＿＿＿＿＿＿＿

(C) acid (n) ＿＿＿＿＿＿＿     (G) nutrient (n) ＿＿＿＿＿＿＿

(D) fat (n) ＿＿＿＿＿＿＿     (H) appreciate (v) ＿＿＿＿＿＿＿

**1.** He bought the low ＿＿＿＿＿ margarine.

**2.** Fruits and vegetables are full of ＿＿＿＿＿s that your body needs.

**3.** We should ＿＿＿＿＿ the fact that we can live in good health every day.

# UNIT 3

# Environment (1)

## 1. Listening Comprehension

Listening Section では，音声から一つ一つの単語を認識していかなければなりません．いわゆる「ローマ字読み」で単語を覚えてしまっていたために，実際にある単語に遭遇した際にその単語だと認識できなかったらもったいないことです．この Unit の Warm up の単語はそれぞれどのように発音するでしょうか．単に意味を覚えるだけではなく，発音，コロケーション，類語など，様々な側面から語彙知識を質的にも量的にも拡大していきましょう．

 *Warm up*

英語に対応する日本語を選びましょう．

1. ecosystem      (  )    a. 産出する
2. pesticide      (  )    b. 生態系
3. agriculture    (  )    c. 殺虫剤
4. yield          (  )    d. 農業

 *Listening Exercises (1)*   1-11〜13

Part A と同じ形式の問題を解きましょう．この Part は，短い会話とそれに続く 1 つの質問から成ります．質問に対する最も適切な解答をそれぞれ (A)–(D) から選びましょう．

1. (A) She is a member of a club.
   (B) She works part time.
   (C) She is in the hospital.
   (D) She had a big fight with her family.

2. (A) She finished only one homework assignment.
   (B) She has one homework assignment left.
   (C) She didn't do any homework.
   (D) Writing reports is her purpose in life.

3. (A) Go buy a smartphone
   (B) Have her smartphone repaired
   (C) Pick up her smartphone from the water
   (D) Go to the station to buy a pass

17

### Listening Exercises (2)  🎧 1-14, 15

Part C と同じ形式の問題を解きましょう．この Part は，長めの講義・スピーチとそれに続く複数の質問から成ります．質問に対する最も適切な解答をそれぞれ (A)–(D) から選びましょう．

1. (A) To give an outline of the course
   (B) To give an outline of pesticides
   (C) To give a basic understanding of the history of agriculture
   (D) To give a brief explanation of harmful insects

2. (A) To combat infectious diseases
   (B) To cultivate insects which benefit agriculture
   (C) To kill cockroaches at home
   (D) To increase agricultural productivity

3. (A) As an example of a substitute for agricultural pesticides
   (B) As an example of an effective method of killing pests
   (C) As an example of a way to increase agricultural productivity
   (D) As an example of something that damages crop yields

4. (A) Alternative ways to increase agricultural productivity
   (B) The battle between humans and pests
   (C) Specific examples of pesticides that could damage the environment
   (D) Specific examples of pesticides currently being used by farmers

### Vocabulary Building (Section 1)

このセクションに登場した単語を辞書で調べ，意味を書きましょう．また，調べた単語を使って，英文を完成させましょう．

(A) toxic       (adj) _____       (D) annually    (adv) _____
(B) centipede   (n) _____         (E) threaten    (adj) _____
(C) bacteria    (n) _____         (F) chemical    (n) _____

1. The whole food chain was affected by the overuse of a _____ in agriculture.
2. Some mushrooms in the park can be _____ to pets.
3. We only meet once a year. Our meeting is held _____.

18

UNIT 3 | Environment (1)

# 2. Structure and Written Expression

豊富な語彙力は, 必ず得点アップに結びつきます. また, 実際の英語運用能力にとっても重要です. TOEFL ITP という点では, 特に学術的な語彙に注目しましょう. フラッシュカードや語彙学習アプリを活用して学習するのがよいでしょう. また, 覚えた単語を実際に使ってみることで, 記憶に定着しやすくなります.

## Warm up

英語に対応する日本語を選びましょう.

| | | | |
|---|---|---|---|
| 1. meteorite | ( ) | a. | 周りの |
| 2. surrounding | ( ) | b. | 隕石 |
| 3. extinction | ( ) | c. | 生物多様性 |
| 4. biodiversity | ( ) | d. | 絶滅 |

## Structure Exercises

空欄に入る最も適切な語句を (A)–(D) から選び, 英文を完成させましょう.

1. The "heat island phenomenon" refers to the situation _____ cities are warmer than the surrounding areas due to man-made heat and pollution.

   (A) which
   (B) of
   (C) where
   (D) in

2. Even though many people believe that meteorite impacts caused the dinosaurs' _____, some argue that the real cause was climate change.

   (A) extinction
   (B) preservation
   (C) suggestion
   (D) prevention

3. We are constantly faced with the issue of food quantity and quality, and this problem is not likely to be _____.

   (A) an easy one to solve
   (B) an easy solution
   (C) a way of solving
   (D) solving easily

4. Climate change, along with other factors, has been cited as a major cause of the mammoth's extinction, which _____ the doom of some other species.

   (A) will have depended
   (B) would have depended
   (C) will have determined
   (D) would have determined

5. While there is an urgent need to
   address issues such as global
   population growth and poverty in
   developing countries, the possibility of
   _____ immediately is quite low.

   (A) they are solved
   (B) them being solved
   (C) them solved
   (D) they solve

6. It has been pointed out that the
   Thwaites Glacier in Antarctica _____
   approximately 50 billion tons of ice
   every year.

   (A) is losing
   (B) will have lost
   (C) had been lost
   (D) is lost

7. We are witnessing a decline in
   biodiversity, _____ the loss of habitat
   caused by land development,
   expansion of agricultural land, and
   excessive grazing.

   (A) with one of the reasons being
   (B) one of the reasons are
   (C) one of the reasons of being
   (D) being one of the reasons

## Written Expression Exercises

英文中の誤った箇所を (A)–(D) から選びましょう.

1. Various <u>approaches</u> have been <u>proposed</u> to solve environmental problems, but economic
        **A**          **B**
   and political factors <u>have prevented</u> them from <u>thoroughly implemented</u> on a global
            **C**             **D**
   scale.

2. Evidence <u>that</u> large-scale climate change <u>prior to</u> the Pleistocene <u>was</u> <u>discovered</u> by
        **A**               **B**      **C**    **D**
   researchers.

3. The Egyptian civilization <u>was founded</u> in a desert area, and the most important factor
                 **A**
   <u>that</u> made it <u>possibly</u> was the presence of a large river <u>nearby</u>.
   **B**     **C**               **D**

4. <u>Since</u> the climate system can be influenced by <u>many variable elements</u>, it is dangerous to
   **A**                 **B**
   discuss <u>them</u> in terms of simple <u>causality</u>.
      **C**           **D**

UNIT 3 Environment (1)

5. The severe flood, <u>which caused</u> substantial damage when <u>it has hit</u> entire villages,
                 **A**                                   **B**
   <u>left behind</u> a scene of <u>extensive destruction and great sadness</u>.
      **C**                   **D**

6. Controlling the <u>flow water</u> has been one of <u>the most</u> important issues <u>throughout</u> human
                 **A**                   **B**                 **C**
   <u>history</u>.
   **D**

7. Solar energy, <u>a renewable resource</u>, can be <u>used directly</u> in different places through
                  **A**                  **B**
   technologies like solar panels, <u>concentrating</u> solar power, and <u>solar building designs</u>.
                             **C**                           **D**

## *Vocabulary Building* (Section 2)

> このセクションに登場した単語を辞書で調べ, 意味を書きましょう. また, 調べた単語を使って,
> 英文を完成させましょう.

(A) doom    (n) _____     (D) grazing    (n) _____

(B) address    (v) _____     (E) implement    (v) _____

(C) witness    (v) _____     (F) archaeologist    (n) _____

1. The city mayor agreed to a plan to _____ the issue of homelessness in the major city centers.

2. We will _____ significant growth in revenue.

3. The _____ of cattle helps maintain grassland health.

## 3. Reading Comprehension

今回は少しずつ時間を意識して解いてみましょう．まずは質問文に素早く目を通して，どんなことが尋ねられているのかを確認しましょう．10−11分で解答できることが望ましいですが，まずは15分くらいで解答することを目指しましょう．

### Warm up

英語に対応する日本語を選びましょう．

| | | | |
|---|---|---|---|
| 1. collapse | ( ) | a. | 干ばつ |
| 2. drought | ( ) | b. | 消滅する |
| 3. vanish | ( ) | c. | 崩壊 |
| 4. flora | ( ) | d. | 耐性 |
| 5. shrub | ( ) | e. | 低木 |
| 6. tolerance | ( ) | f. | 植物相 |

### Reading Exercises

次の文章を読み，下の問いに対する最も適切な解答をそれぞれ (A)−(D) から選びましょう．

The decline of the ancient Mayan civilization was probably not solely caused by drought. Around the end of the ninth century, a series of droughts in the area that is now known as southeastern Mexico and northern Central America caused severe hardship for this powerful culture, one of the earliest in Mesoamerica.

5　　　Research has shown that Mayan societies vanished mysteriously during this time. Since the Mayan people relied heavily on drought-sensitive products such as maize, corn, beans, and squash, it is believed that the droughts caused widespread hunger.

The researchers who recently conducted the study discovered that the Mayans had access to a large variety of 497 local food plant species. The drought tolerance of a particular
10　plant or a certain environment is often the subject of research. Examining the dietary flora of an entire civilization, including a large range of plant species, both wild and domesticated, was what made this study unique.

The researchers created a list of indigenous Mayan food plants by drawing from earlier research on Mayan plant use. In light of the widespread belief that drought was the root of
15　Mayan societal unrest, they chose to evaluate each plant's tolerance to drought. For the majority of the edible plants that would be available during a year of normal rainfall, they identified edible portions such as fruits and roots. A few of the food plant species' specific edible components were not recognized. Fifty-nine types of edible plants would have probably survived, even in the worst drought conditions.

20　　　The hardiest plants the Mayans would have used include hearts of palm and cassava, which have edible tubers. Another significant plant is a shrub that was tamed by the Mayans and whose present-day descendants still eat its calcium-, iron-, potassium-, and protein-rich

22

leaves. These plants might have served as a substantial source of protein and carbohydrates.

Although the researchers were unable to determine the precise reason why the Mayan civilization collapsed, they contend that the effects of social and economic dislocation should not be undervalued. They contend that it is probably inaccurate to assume that a drought will cause an agricultural collapse.

They (the researchers) emphasize how crucial it is to use a wide variety of plants for drought tolerance and climate change mitigation. Maintaining a variety of drought-resistant crops could help cultures, both ancient and modern, adapt and endure even in the face of a series of droughts.

1. What is the main point of the passage?
   (A) Cassava was found to be rich in nutrition.
   (B) Drought was the main cause of the end of Mayan civilization.
   (C) It is impossible to resist climate change.
   (D) The reasons for the disappearance of the Mayan civilization are complex.

2. The word "indigenous" in line 13 is closest in meaning to
   (A) agricultural
   (B) developed
   (C) modern
   (D) native

3. The word "unrest" in line 15 is closest in meaning to
   (A) dependence
   (B) disruption
   (C) identification
   (D) inclusion

4. According to the passage, which statement is NOT true?
   (A) Researchers agree that Mayan societies began to disappear at the end of the ninth century.
   (B) The researchers examine the drought tolerance of almost 500 plants.
   (C) Heart of palm is high in carbohydrates and protein.
   (D) The descendants of the Maya have stopped eating cassava.

5. What did the researchers find regarding the drought tolerance of the edible plants available to the Mayans?
   (A) Almost 60 edible plants could likely withstand severe drought.
   (B) None of the edible plants showed any tolerance to drought.
   (C) The bulk of the plants could survive in the worst drought conditions.
   (D) The researchers were unable to determine the drought tolerance of the edible plants.

**6.** What is the significance of the shrub mentioned in the passage?

(A) It is a drought-tolerant plant.

(B) It is a source of protein and carbohydrates for the Mayans.

(C) It played a role in the Mayan society's collapse.

(D) Its leaves are rich in calcium, iron, and potassium.

**7.** Which of the following best describes the researchers' view on the role of drought in the collapse of Mayan civilization?

(A) Drought had no significant impact on the collapse.

(B) Drought was a contributing factor, but not the main cause, of the collapse.

(C) Drought was the sole cause of the collapse.

(D) The researchers did not express a clear opinion on the role of drought.

**8.** What do the researchers emphasize as a key strategy for adapting to climate change and droughts?

(A) Finding alternative water sources during droughts

(B) Implementing strict water conservation measures

(C) Relying on a single drought-resistant crop for sustenance

(D) Using a wide variety of plants for drought tolerance

## *Vocabulary Building* (Section 3)

> このセクションに登場した単語を辞書で調べ，意味を書きましょう．また，調べた単語を使って，英文を完成させましょう．

(A) conduct  (v) ＿＿＿＿＿＿＿  (E) tame  (v) ＿＿＿＿＿＿＿

(B) domesticated  (adj) ＿＿＿＿＿＿＿  (F) contend  (v) ＿＿＿＿＿＿＿

(C) edible  (adj) ＿＿＿＿＿＿＿  (G) assume  (v) ＿＿＿＿＿＿＿

(D) tuber  (n) ＿＿＿＿＿＿＿

**1.** Dogs are ＿＿＿＿＿ animals that have been living with humans for thousands of years.

**2.** It is difficult for ordinary people to distinguish between ＿＿＿＿＿ and poisonous mushrooms.

**3.** He managed to ＿＿＿＿＿ his fear of public speaking through practice.

# UNIT 4

# Science and Technology (1)

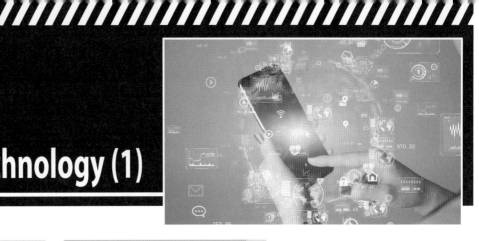

## 1. Listening Comprehension

Section B ではやや長めの会話を聞きます．教授と学生，学生どうし，図書館司書と学生などのパターンがあります．大学生活で起こり得る様々な状況が取り上げられますので，学問分野に関するものや，大学での日常生活に関連するものなど，幅広い語彙に対応しなければなりません．この Unit では学生新聞の記者が大学教授にインタビューを行います．この場合は，インタビューの目的を捉え，教授の専門分野を推測できるよう注意して聞きましょう．

 **Warm up**

英語に対応する日本語を選びましょう．

1. diversity       (   )    a. 特徴
2. feature         (   )    b. 交通機関
3. anthropology    (   )    c. 多様性
4. transportation  (   )    d. 人類学

 **Listening Exercises (1)**  CD 1-16〜18

Part A と同じ形式の問題を解きましょう．この Part は，短い会話とそれに続く1つの質問から成ります．質問に対する最も適切な解答をそれぞれ (A)–(D) から選びましょう．

1. (A) The woman should join the baseball team.
   (B) The man will ask the woman's friends if they would like to join.
   (C) The woman's friend will introduce potential members.
   (D) The number of people interested in the sport is decreasing.

2. (A) He knows the way to the classroom.
   (B) He attends the same class as the woman.
   (C) He wants to find out where her classroom is.
   (D) He doesn't have a class in the afternoon.

3. (A) The friend is waiting for him at the library.
   (B) The friend works at the stationery store.
   (C) The friend is about to have a birthday party.
   (D) The friend met him for the first time at the stationery store.

### Listening Exercises (2)　CD 1-19, 20

Part B と同じ形式の問題を解きましょう. この Part は, 長めの会話とそれに続く複数の質問から成ります.
質問に対する最も適切な解答をそれぞれ (A)–(D) から選びましょう.

1. (A) A student interviews a professor about the contents of a book she has published.
   (B) A student asks a musician to teach him how to become a street musician.
   (C) A student asks a professor questions about the history of the Métro.
   (D) A student and a professor discuss joint research on Parisian culture.

2. (A) In 1997
   (B) 20 years before
   (C) Last year
   (D) The year before last

3. (A) The musician introduced in the case became famous.
   (B) The agency that operates public transport promoted the book.
   (C) The professor appeared on TV and introduced the book to the general public.
   (D) The book won a competition for academic books.

4. (A) 10 candidates
   (B) 20 candidates
   (C) 200 candidates
   (D) 2,000 candidates

### Vocabulary Building (Section 1)

このセクションに登場した単語を辞書で調べ, 意味を書きましょう. また, 調べた単語を使って,
英文を完成させましょう.

(A) audition　(n) _____　(D) aspect　(n) _____
(B) evolve　(v) _____　(E) spotlight　(n) _____
(C) along with　(prep) _____　(F) progression　(n) _____

1. Poetic forms share a small part with the musical _____ of poetry.
2. The conclusion was a natural _____ from the previous parts of the story.
3. The new publication has thrown the _____ on technological developments.

UNIT 4 Science and Technology (1)

## 2. Structure and Written Expression

学術英語でよく用いられる文法項目は特に重点的に学習したいものです．関係代名詞，仮定法，分詞構文，受動態などは，試験でも頻繁に出題されます．各文法項目の基本ルールだけでなく，例外や注意点も確認しましょう．理解が曖昧な部分は，参考書や信頼できるウェブサイトなどで調べるのもよいでしょう．

### Warm up

英語に対応する日本語を選びましょう．

1. function （　　）  **a.** 機能
2. advance （　　）  **b.** 後の
3. subsequent （　　）  **c.** 前に進める
4. utilize （　　）  **d.** 利用する

### Structure Exercises

空欄に入る最も適切な語句を (A)–(D) から選び，英文を完成させましょう．

1. Steam engines transform the thermal energy from steam into _____ force.

   (A) rotational
   (B) rotation
   (C) rotates
   (D) rotated

2. Some engines guide steam into a cylinder, _____ others use steam to turn a turbine.

   (A) because
   (B) while
   (C) therefore
   (D) such as

3. Heron's aeolipile, _____ by Heron of ancient Alexandria, marked a significant turning point.

   (A) designing
   (B) designed
   (C) to design
   (D) having designed

4. Electric power generation _____ converting energy sources into electricity, often through turbines driven by steam or water flow, wind, or gas.

   (A) involves
   (B) preserves
   (C) retains
   (D) pertains

27

5. Thomas Savery, _____ work was trailblazing, presented the "fire engine" in 1698.

(A) whose
(B) who's
(C) which
(D) whom

6. If Thomas Newcomen _____ not discovered his method, the development of steam engines might have been delayed.

(A) would
(B) was
(C) had
(D) did

7. Newcomen's steam engine is seen as the _____ that powered the subsequent Industrial Revolution.

(A) icing on the cake
(B) feather in the cap
(C) driving force
(D) last straw

## Written Expression Exercises

英文中の誤った箇所を (A)–(D) から選びましょう.

1. James Watt, a <u>distinguishing</u> engineer <u>from</u> Scotland, revolutionized mechanical
                **A**           **B**
   engineering <u>by introducing</u> an innovative steam engine in 1769, <u>setting</u> the stage for
           **C**                                    **D**
   future industrial advancements.

2. In 1766, Watt became a land <u>surveyor</u>, and <u>in</u> the next eight years, he was busy <u>to map</u>
                           **A**        **B**                       **C**
   canal routes in Scotland, which slowed down his <u>work on</u> the steam engine.
                                              **D**

3. The concept <u>to utilizing</u> the force of steam <u>to spin</u> a turbine is not a recent innovation; it
             **A**                     **B**
   has <u>deep</u> historical roots that <u>span over</u> centuries.
       **C**                **D**

4. In 1882, Gustaf de Laval developed <u>the idea of</u> an <u>impulse</u> steam turbine, and by 1887,
                                 **A**     **B**
   he <u>has demonstrated</u> that it was possible to construct a <u>smaller</u> version of it.
       **C**                                    **D**

**5.** Sir Charles Parsons from the UK, is a pioneering figure in the history of mechanical
                                    **A**
 engineering, was notably the first individual to construct a large-scale turbine, laying the
            **B**                                                      **C**
 groundwork for future developments in turbine technology.
                  **D**

**6.** Even in today's rapidly advancing technological age, steam turbines retain their
    **A**
 relevance, holding significant importance and prominently utilized across a wide range of
           **B**                                  **C**                    **D**
 applications in various industries.

**7.** Water is heated in a boiler to create steam, which spins the turbine blades, and is then
         **A**                                 **B**
 cooled back into water to be reuse for more steam.
                **C**     **D**

## *Vocabulary Building* (Section 2)

> このセクションに登場した単語を辞書で調べ, 意味を書きましょう. また, 調べた単語を使って,
> 英文を完成させましょう.

(A) trailblazing   (adj) _____     (D) continent   (n) _____
(B) lasting         (adj) _____     (E) construct   (v) _____
(C) alternately   (adv) _____     (F) retain     (v) _____

**1.** The scientist's _____ research led to new treatments.
**2.** Africa is a diverse _____ , rich in culture, wildlife, and natural beauty.
**3.** Students use flashcards to _____ information more effectively before the exam.

# 3. Reading Comprehension

Reading Section は 55 分でパッセージを 5 つ読む必要があるので，1 パッセージを 10–11 分で終わらせる必要があります．全体の主旨を問う，具体的な情報を探す，単語の意味を問う，筆者の意図を問う問題などです．いずれも本文の中に必ず答えを 1 つに絞る根拠があります．

## Warm up

英語に対応する日本語を選びましょう．

| | | | | |
|---|---|---|---|---|
| **1.** infrastructure | ( ) | **a.** 即応性・応答 |
| **2.** iteration | ( ) | **b.** 統合・統一 |
| **3.** transmission | ( ) | **c.** 通信・伝達 |
| **4.** responsiveness | ( ) | **d.** 基盤・基礎 |
| **5.** integration | ( ) | **e.** バージョン・版 |

## Reading Exercises

次の文章を読み，下の問いに対する最も適切な解答をそれぞれ (A)–(D) から選びましょう．

5G technology represents the recent technological trend. While you may have some familiarity with the term, its significance and meaning may not be immediately apparent. 5G stands for the fifth iteration of mobile network infrastructure. Successive advancements from 1G to 2G have led to increased performance and functionality. Currently, the emergence of 5G
5  technology has introduced unprecedented levels of speed and functionality.

One exceptional feature of 5G technology is its rapid transmission rate. Moreover, it allows for the download of a full-length movie in mere seconds. Additionally, those who have faced interruptions while participating in video calls or playing games online will appreciate the improved reactivity that 5G technology ensures, making online interactions more seamless
10  thanks to reduced latency, which is particularly beneficial for real-time communication.

Beyond improved speed and responsiveness, 5G technology will enable an expanded range of connectivity. 5G aims to connect multiple devices simultaneously and usher in a new era of interconnectivity among cars, appliances, and phones. The development of a reliable and fast infrastructure is precisely what 5G technology will provide.

15  It is worth noting, however, that despite its promising potential, 5G has yet to be widely adopted on a global level. While certain geographic regions have welcomed this innovative technology, the majority remains unfamiliar with its benefits. Although its implementation is expected to expand in the upcoming years, safety concerns still persist. On the other hand, experts claim that 5G is just as safe for widespread integration as its predecessor.

20  The emergence of 5G marks a milestone in technological history. Its predicted integration into our daily life is expected to result in significant changes in the way we communicate and understand it. 5G will undoubtedly pave the way for a bright future.

30

**1.** What is the main idea of the passage?

(A) Features and benefits of 5G technology

(B) History and development of 5G technology

(C) Safety and challenges of 5G technology

(D) Applications and future potential of 5G technology

**2.** What will be an effect of the increased speeds brought about by 5G technology?

(A) Faster movie download times

(B) Uninterrupted video calls and online games

(C) Smoother real-time communication

(D) All of the above

**3.** What does "unprecedented levels of speed and functionality" in line 5 mean?

(A) Unmatched speed and capabilities

(B) Speeds and features that have never been seen before

(C) Speeds and features that are better than previous generations

(D) Speeds and features that are only available in certain geographic regions

**4.** The word "latency" in line 10 is closest in meaning to

(A) speed

(B) functionality

(C) delay

(D) cost

**5.** Why does the author mention the difficulty of downloading a full-length movie in the second paragraph?

(A) To compare 5G speeds to those of previous generations

(B) To emphasize the benefits of 5G for streaming and downloading content

(C) To highlight the need for a reliable and fast infrastructure

(D) To discuss the potential drawbacks of 5G technology

**6.** What are some of the obstacles to the widespread availability of 5G technology?

(A) Geographic restrictions

(B) Safety concerns

(C) Technical difficulties

(D) Both (A) and (B)

7. What areas will 5G technology revolutionize?
   (A) Electricity and electronics
   (B) Communication and understanding
   (C) The short- and long-term future
   (D) All of the above

8. 5G technology is both promising and challenging. What are some of the potential benefits and drawbacks of 5G technology?
   (A) Benefits: Increased speed, improved responsiveness, expanded range of connectivity; Drawbacks: Safety concerns
   (B) Benefits: Improved responsiveness, expanded range of connectivity; Drawbacks: Safety concerns
   (C) Benefits: Increased speed, expanded range of connectivity; Drawbacks: Limited global adoption
   (D) Benefits: Increased speed, improved responsiveness; Drawbacks: Limited global adoption, safety concerns

## *Vocabulary Building* (Section 3)

> このセクションに登場した単語を辞書で調べ, 意味を書きましょう. また, 調べた単語を使って, 英文を完成させましょう.

(A) unprecedented (adj) _____    (D) reactivity (n) _____
(B) ensure (v) _____    (E) interconnectivity (n) _____
(C) seamless (adj) _____

1. The COVID-19 pandemic was a(n) _____ event that changed the world forever.
2. 5G technology makes online interactions more _____.
3. The 5G network will enable _____ between different devices, such as cars, appliances, and phones.

# UNIT 5

# Biology (1)

## 1. Listening Comprehension

Part C は，大学の講義の一部から出題されることが多い部分です．長く，またやや専門的な内容が含まれることもありますので，最後まで話題の流れを追えるように転換語等に注意しながらメモをとっていきましょう．この Unit には，近代の生物の話，考古学的な生物の話など，複数の話題が含まれ，話題が転換するタイミングがあります．話題の転換を意識して聞き取り，どのような転換語とともに話題が変わったのかをメモしましょう．

### Warm up

英語に対応する日本語を選びましょう.

1. respiration　　　（　　）　　a. 染料
2. archaeology　　（　　）　　b. 特徴的な
3. distinctive　　　（　　）　　c. 呼吸
4. dye　　　　　　（　　）　　d. 考古学

### Listening Exercises (1)  1-21〜23

Part A と同じ形式の問題を解きましょう．この Part は，短い会話とそれに続く1つの質問から成ります．質問に対する最も適切な解答をそれぞれ (A)–(D) から選びましょう．

1. (A) The woman is open to eating take-out meals.
   (B) The woman is looking for a job in the food industry.
   (C) The woman cooks her own meals every day.
   (D) The woman works for a frozen food company.

2. (A) Give the ticket to the woman
   (B) Go to the theater with the woman
   (C) Visit his sick friend
   (D) Buy a new ticket

3. (A) There is no need to submit the homework.
   (B) The deadline for the homework has already passed.
   (C) It is not allowed to have someone else submit the homework.
   (D) No homework has been assigned.

33

### Listening Exercises (2)  CD 1-24, 25

Part C と同じ形式の問題を解きましょう．この Part は，長めの講義・スピーチとそれに続く複数の質問から成ります．質問に対する最も適切な解答をそれぞれ (A)–(D) から選びましょう．

1. (A) How to find out what color dinosaurs were
   (B) How to tell if dinosaurs resembled modern birds
   (C) How to efficiently discover well-preserved fossils
   (D) Species of carrots eaten by dinosaurs in movies

2. (A) Because the color of crows appears to shimmer depending on the angle
   (B) To show that crows have better brains than humans
   (C) Because the color of crows has changed over time
   (D) Because analyzing crow skeletons will advance dinosaur research

3. (A) They contained the same pigments as carrots.
   (B) They lived in extremely hot areas near a volcano.
   (C) They flew in the sky like modern birds.
   (D) It is not known whether they were actually red.

4. (A) By examining the entire body of the dinosaur under a microscope
   (B) By inferring from the pigments found in a part of the body
   (C) By considering the characteristics of the place where they lived
   (D) By asking an artist to make his or her best guess

### Vocabulary Building (Section 1)

> このセクションに登場した単語を辞書で調べ，意味を書きましょう．また，調べた単語を使って，英文を完成させましょう．

(A) mammal      (n) _____      (D) substance   (n) _____
(B) microscope  (n) _____      (E) investigate (v) _____
(C) angle       (n) _____      (F) vibrant     (adj) _____

1. A lion is a _____ native to the savannah.
2. Scientists could _____ tigers' ecology long before modern technology developed.
3. The plant seems to emit a(n) _____ that makes people uncomfortable.

34

UNIT 5 Biology (1)

## 2. Structure and Written Expression

問題集を活用して，試験形式に慣れることが重要です．実際の試験と同じ形式の問題を解くことで，時間配分や解答のコツをつかむことができます．間違えた問題に関連する文法・語法はすぐに調べましょう．同じミスを繰り返さないために，間違いの原因を分析し，対策を立てることが大切です．

### Warm up

英語に対応する日本語を選びましょう．

1. migratory    (  )    a. 解剖学的に
2. nocturnal    (  )    b. 特徴
3. anatomically (  )    c. 移動性の
4. trait        (  )    d. 夜間の

### Structure Exercises

空欄に入る最も適切な語句を (A)–(D) から選び，英文を完成させましょう．

1. It is remarkable that a lot of birds, despite their small size, have the _____ to fly over vast distances spanning thousands of kilometers.

   (A) capability
   (B) reliability
   (C) method
   (D) technique

2. Scholars have stressed the _____ of radar technology in analyzing the nocturnal flight patterns of migratory birds.

   (A) formation
   (B) effectiveness
   (C) utility
   (D) usage

3. If birds _____ not evolved both anatomically and physiologically, they might not be able to undertake long journeys in the sky.

   (A) had
   (B) did
   (C) does
   (D) were to

4. The methodologies that _____ used to investigate the movements of migratory birds have been significantly improved by the recent advancements in radar technology.

   (A) are
   (B) is
   (C) was
   (D) have

35

5. Migratory birds often have varying behaviors and habitats, _____ on their species, the season, and the geographical region.

(A) depends
(B) depend
(C) depending
(D) depended

6. Birds, _____ evolved both anatomically and physiologically, are capable of going on long journeys in the sky.

(A) have
(B) having
(C) had
(D) to have

7. The quest for suitable breeding or nesting sites is _____ that many animals exhibit.

(A) which
(B) what
(C) something
(D) ones

## Written Expression Exercises

英文中の誤った箇所を (A)–(D) から選びましょう.

1. Living in mild and calm places <u>during</u> <u>the time</u> they don't breed <u>help</u> animals live <u>longer</u>.
   <br>                                    **A**     **B**                      **C**         **D**

2. <u>Since</u> the dawn of human history, birds and people <u>have formed</u> a deep and <u>enduring</u>
   <br>   **A**                                             **B**              **C**
   <br>connection, <u>show</u> our bond with nature.
   <br>             **D**

3. <u>With</u> the advancement of modern techniques for studying genes, researchers are gaining
   <br>  **A**
   <br>fresh insights <u>on</u> the <u>various</u> species of birds and further exploring their
   <br>              **B**    **C**
   <br><u>evolutionary history</u>.
   <br>     **D**

4. Researchers and paleontologists <u>specialize</u> <u>in</u> examining ancient bones <u>argue</u> <u>that</u> to truly
   <br>                                   **A**  **B**                          **C**  **D**
   <br>comprehend the detailed aspects of dinosaur life and evolution, it's essential to
   <br>understand bird life.

5. <u>Despite</u> of the common knowledge that humans <u>belong</u> to the category of mammals, it's
   <br>  **A**                                                **B**
   <br>quite <u>surprising</u> to discover just how many parallels and similarities <u>we share</u> with birds.
   <br>       **C**                                                 **D**

UNIT 5　Biology (1)

6. Similarly to our understanding that monkeys utilize tools in their daily activities, it's
   　　　A　　　　　　　　　　B
   fascinating to observe that certain bird species also possess this capability.
   　　　　　　　　　　　　C　　　　　　　　　　D

7. One of the traits shared among mammals, birds, and some dinosaurs is the capacity to
   　　　　　　　　　　　A　　　　　　　　　　　　　　　　　　　　B　　　　　　　　C
   regulate and maintain a body temperature that is raised compare to the external
   　　　　　　　　　　　　　　　　　　　　　　　　　　D
   environment.

## Vocabulary Building (Section 2)

> このセクションに登場した単語を辞書で調べ, 意味を書きましょう. また, 調べた単語を使って,
> 英文を完成させましょう.

(A) remarkable　(adj) ＿＿＿＿＿＿＿　(D) suitable　(adj) ＿＿＿＿＿＿＿

(B) stress　(v) ＿＿＿＿＿＿＿　(E) insight　(n) ＿＿＿＿＿＿＿

(C) vary　(v) ＿＿＿＿＿＿＿　(F) similarly　(adv) ＿＿＿＿＿＿＿

1. Please ＿＿＿＿＿ the important parts of the text in your slides.
2. This recipe is ＿＿＿＿＿ for vegetarians because it doesn't contain any meat.
3. Her book provides profound ＿＿＿＿＿ into the challenges of modern society.

# 3. Reading Comprehension

Reading Section は本文に明確に書いてあることが問われるとは限りません．ある文章の書かれた目的や，筆者の考えを推測する問題も含まれます．文章の内容をきちんと理解していれば解ける問題ばかりですが，設問パターンを理解していないと必要以上に時間をかけてしまうので注意が必要です．

## Warm up

英語に対応する日本語を選びましょう．

1. sustenance     (   )     **a.** 家畜
2. cultivation     (   )     **b.** 区別・差別化
3. differentiation   (   )     **c.** 検査・調査
4. inspection     (   )     **d.** 食物・食糧
5. livestock     (   )     **e.** 培養・栽培

## Reading Exercises

次の文章を読み，下の問いに対する最も適切な解答をそれぞれ (A)–(D) から選びましょう．

Over time, our perspective on sustenance has evolved. One topic of interest is the emergence of "cultured meat," which is produced in scientific laboratories rather than on a farm. Through the cultivation of animal cells in an optimal environment, these cells undergo growth and differentiation into the physical structure that we recognize as meat. Authentic
5 meat, which has been cultivated through a special process rather than being imitation meat from plants, is having a great impact on our food history.

In contrast, the meat that has been conventionally consumed for decades comes from animals, such as pigs, poultry, and cows, that are directly sourced from farms. Conventionally, the animals consumed are reared on farms that directly supply the meat we eat.

10 These two types of meat differ in their respective manufacturing procedures. Cultured meat produced in a laboratory is a technological innovation, whereas natural meat originates from traditional agriculture. In terms of environmental impact, laboratory-grown meat is preferable since it requires less land and water, emits fewer greenhouse gases and, in some cases, requires fewer resources than common livestock production methods that are
15 environmentally damaging.

From a health and safety perspective, laboratory-grown meat reduces the risk of diseases that may originate from farms by ensuring a controlled environment. Nevertheless, safety inspections are carried out on both types of meat before they are delivered to consumers. While there may be slight differences in flavor and texture between laboratory-
20 grown and natural meat, technological advancements are making them more consistent. Some people who have eaten lab-grown meat argue that it is similar to traditional meat.

The increasing demand for cultured meat in the market and on dining tables is

38

unsurprising. This pioneering approach towards producing meat in a more ecologically sustainable way demonstrates human creativity. However, the attraction to natural meat is still remarkably strong. An individual's awareness of where their food comes from helps them to make informed choices.

25

1. What is the main idea of this passage?
   (A) Changing food perspectives and the emergence of cultured meat
   (B) Cultured vs. natural meat production methods and environmental impact
   (C) Taste and health differences between cultured and natural meat
   (D) Market demand and future potential for cultured meat

2. How is cultured meat produced?
   (A) By using a special process to create imitation meat from plants
   (B) By culturing animal cells in an optimal environment to form the meat structure
   (C) By scientifically processing the meat of farmed animals
   (D) By using genetic engineering techniques to create new types of meat

3. What are the differences between cultured meat and natural meat mentioned in the third paragraph of the passage?
   (A) Production method and environmental impact
   (B) Taste and texture
   (C) Safety and quality
   (D) Price and availability

4. What is a benefit of cultured meat from an environmental perspective?
   (A) It requires less land.
   (B) It requires less water.
   (C) It emits fewer greenhouse gases.
   (D) All of the above

5. What is a drawback of cultured meat?
   (A) It is currently more expensive.
   (B) It has a slightly different taste.
   (C) It has a slightly different texture.
   (D) Both (B) and (C)

6. According to the passage, what is one of the advantages of cultured meat for health and safety?
   (A) Reduced risk of possible farm-borne diseases
   (B) Safety inspections before delivery to consumers
   (C) Technological advances that ensure consistency of taste and texture
   (D) Claims that it is similar to traditional meat

**7.** What is the most probable reason for the growing demand for cultured meat?

(A) People are becoming more concerned about the environmental impact of meat production.

(B) People are becoming more concerned about the health and safety of meat production.

(C) People are becoming more concerned about the cost of meat production.

(D) All of the above

**8.** What is the author's prediction for the future of cultured meat?

(A) Cultured meat will become more popular.

(B) Cultured meat will become less expensive.

(C) Cultured meat will become more commonly available.

(D) All of the above

## Vocabulary Building (Section 3)

> このセクションに登場した単語を辞書で調べ，意味を書きましょう．また，調べた単語を使って，英文を完成させましょう．

(A) authentic   (adj) _____   (D) sustainable   (adj) _____

(B) respective   (adj) _____   (E) awareness   (n) _____

(C) preferable   (adj) _____

**1.** These two types of food products differ in their _____ manufacturing procedures.

**2.** Laboratory-grown meat is _____ .

**3.** Cultured meat is a new and innovative way to produce meat that is more environmentally friendly and _____ than conventional methods.

# UNIT 6

## Art (1)

### 1. Listening Comprehension

この Unit では講義形式で芸術を取り上げます．絵画分野で身に付けておくべき背景知識としては，有名な画家やその代表作，○○派・○○主義などの分類名とその概略などです．それぞれ，英語で何と言うかをできる限り把握しておくことに努めましょう．Listening Exercise (2) では『ひまわり』で有名なゴッホが出てきます．有名な画家に関しては，どのような人生を歩み，それがその人の作品にどう反映されているのかといったことまで出題範囲になり得ます．

### Warm up

英語に対応する日本語を選びましょう．

1. artist　　　　　　（　）　　a. 印象派
2. characterize　　　（　）　　b. 好意的に評価する
3. impressionism　　（　）　　c. 芸術家
4. appreciate　　　　（　）　　d. 特徴づける

### Listening Exercises (1)  1-26〜28

Part A と同じ形式の問題を解きましょう．この Part は，短い会話とそれに続く1つの質問から成ります．質問に対する最も適切な解答をそれぞれ (A)–(D) から選びましょう．

1. (A) The instructor of the class they are taking
   (B) The pilot of the flight they were supposed to take
   (C) A friend of theirs who is taking the same class
   (D) A friend from the man's hometown

2. (A) He didn't go to the beach during summer vacation.
   (B) A soccer tournament is just around the corner.
   (C) He was planning to travel during summer vacation.
   (D) He wants the woman to join the soccer club.

3. (A) He is not able to care for more cats.
   (B) The man's cat also recently had kittens.
   (C) The man is not allowed to keep cats in his house.
   (D) The man is about to adopt a kitten.

41

## Listening Exercises (2)  1-29, 30

Part C と同じ形式の問題を解きましょう．この Part は，長めの講義・スピーチとそれに続く複数の質問から成ります．質問に対する最も適切な解答をそれぞれ (A)–(D) から選びましょう．

1. (A) Thin, delicate brushstrokes
   (B) Bright, neon colors
   (C) Thick, textured paint application
   (D) Black and white color schemes

2. (A) His extensive travels around the world
   (B) His early recognition and fame
   (C) His struggles with mental health
   (D) His formal art education at a young age

3. (A) He wants the students to understand that Van Gogh indeed had challenging times.
   (B) He wants the students to consider how his health issues influenced his works.
   (C) He prefers not to go deep into his health issues.
   (D) He does not intend to give an extensive lecture about impressionism.

4. (A) Cubism
   (B) Renaissance
   (C) Post-Impressionism
   (D) Realism

## Vocabulary Building (Section 1)

> このセクションに登場した単語を辞書で調べ，意味を書きましょう．また，調べた単語を使って，英文を完成させましょう．

(A) unique     (adj) _____     (D) emotion   (n) _____
(B) struggle   (v) _____       (E) touch     (v) _____
(C) conceive   (v) _____       (F) mental    (adj) _____

1. We're going to _____ on an artist, a well-known artist who influenced Western art a lot.
2. His works show us how he would _____ the world.
3. The pen given to an artist by his teacher made his art so _____ .

UNIT 6 | Art (1)

## 2. Structure and Written Expression

間違えた箇所をあつめたノートを作成し，いつでも見返せるようにしましょう．重要なポイントや自分が間違えやすい項目を整理することで，効率よく復習ができるでしょう．図や表，色分けなどを活用して視覚的に印象に残りやすくする工夫をしてもよいですね．ある程度情報があつまってくると，だんだんと自分の苦手なところの傾向がわかってきます．

### Warm up

英語に対応する日本語を選びましょう.

1. curiosity ( ) **a.** 好奇心
2. geographical ( ) **b.** 顕著な
3. prominent ( ) **c.** 地理的な
4. representative ( ) **d.** 代表的な

### Structure Exercises

空欄に入る最も適切な語句を (A)–(D) から選び，英文を完成させましょう.

1. The Arabian region, developed in science and culture, _____ the curiosity of European people.

   (A) sparked
   (B) brought
   (C) interested
   (D) focused

2. Trade in various goods, including spices, became _____ in the Mediterranean region during the time of the Crusades.

   (A) alive
   (B) lively
   (C) living
   (D) to live

3. Some researchers point out that Florence's _____, being surrounded by mountains, contributed to a foundation for cultural uniqueness.

   (A) location
   (B) isolation
   (C) migration
   (D) prescription

4. The Renaissance era saw the emergence of new techniques in various fields, with painting _____ a particularly prominent example.

   (A) is
   (B) to be
   (C) being
   (D) was

43

5. The Reformation is _____ one of the factors that led to the end of the Renaissance era.

   (A) seen
   (B) argued
   (C) mentioned
   (D) considered

6. In "The Last Supper," created in his early to mid-40s, Da Vinci masterfully used _____ to express the emotions of each character with their actions.

   (A) initiative
   (B) relative
   (C) perspective
   (D) captive

7. Michelangelo is known for works such as "David" _____ in the Accademia Gallery in Florence and the "Last Judgment" Fresco in the Sistine Chapel.

   (A) sculptor
   (B) sculpture
   (C) architecture
   (D) architect

## Written Expression Exercises

英文中の誤った箇所を (A)–(D) から選びましょう.

1. The term "Renaissance" in French deriving from the Italian word "rinascimento,"
        **A**            **B**          **C**
   meaning "rebirth" or "revival".
   **D**

2. In Baroque art, dynamic and imbalanced expressions were preferred on the balanced
       **A**             **B**                 **C**
   compositions idealized in the Renaissance period.
             **D**

3. In perspective, there are various techniques including linear perspective, aerial
             **A**               **B**
   perspective softens distant views, and foreshortening that creates depth by shortening
           **C**                   **D**
   motifs.

4. Petrarch is a representative literal figure of the Renaissance, deeply skilled in Latin and
                    **A**                   **B**   **C**
   known for his poetry particularly the "Canzoniere" written in Italian.
           **D**

UNIT 6 Art (1)

**5.** During the Renaissance, intellectuals aimed to understand humanity through the study of
          A                         B                         C
Greek and Roman classics were called humanists.
                             D

**6.** The revival of classic culture in European medieval times around the 12th century is
                  A                      B                                    C
referred to as the 12th Century Renaissance.
           D

**7.** The 12th Century Renaissance was a time when liberal arts education had been
                                  A    B      C                    D
revitalized.

## *Vocabulary Building* (Section 2)

このセクションに登場した単語を辞書で調べ，意味を書きましょう．また，調べた単語を使って，
英文を完成させましょう．

(A) region      (n) _____     (D) isolation     (n) _____
(B) emergence  (n) _____     (E) foundation  (n) _____
(C) linear        (adj) _____   (F) revival      (n) _____

**1.** The _____ of wireless technology in the early 21st century drastically changed how
we communicate and access information.

**2.** The scientist worked in complete _____ to avoid any external influences on her
experiments.

**3.** The charity organization, known for its humanitarian work, was built on the _____ of
compassion and community service.

45

# 3. Reading Comprehension

単語の意味を問う問題では，受験生が知らない可能性の高い単語がよく出題されます．つまり，未知の単語の意味を文脈から推測できるかどうかが問われます．選択肢を文に当てはめ，文意が通るかを慎重に検討しましょう．また普段から未知語があったら単語の意味を調べる前に推測し，その後確認することで語彙力・推測力を向上させることができます．

## Warm up

英語に対応する日本語を選びましょう．

| | | | | |
|---|---|---|---|---|
| **1.** synthetic | ( ) | **a.** 一貫性がない |
| **2.** intuition | ( ) | **b.** 検証 |
| **3.** inconsistent | ( ) | **c.** 合成の |
| **4.** deviate | ( ) | **d.** 懐疑的な見方 |
| **5.** skepticism | ( ) | **e.** 直感 |
| **6.** verification | ( ) | **f.** 外れる，逸脱する |

## Reading Exercises

次の文章を読み，下の問いに対する最も適切な解答をそれぞれ (A)–(D) から選びましょう．

With advancements in technology and particularly the leaps and bounds in the development of artificial intelligence (AI), it is becoming more difficult to determine how much of an image is real and how much of it might have been created by a computer. Determining authenticity is a deceptively difficult task as images produced by artificial
5 intelligence can appear extremely realistic. As AI image processing has become more popular and accessible, there have been an increasing number of photographs that appear genuine but are not. Some websites and applications facilitate the creation of synthetic images, also called "deep fakes," which can be very difficult for people to distinguish as "real" or not.

Despite this, according to a university computer science professor, humans possess
10 unique abilities that enable them to intuitively identify these counterfeit photographs. Using this insight and modelling from human behavior, scientists are investigating methods to instruct computers how to identify fake photographs in the same way humans do.

Intuition plays a crucial role in distinguishing between "real" images and those generated by AI. Images may seem peculiar or inconsistent. There may be slight irregularities
15 such as hair, eyewear, jewelry, hand placements that deviate from the norm, or peculiarities in eye shapes and reflections. There may, as well, be the odd play of light and shadow. Despite not being able to explain why, people, more than computers, are much more sensitive to such flaws.

With the growth of AI generated images, it is wise to maintain an appropriate degree
20 of skepticism toward the media and to authenticate an image's source and accuracy prior to adopting it as true. Image searches and other online tools can go a long way to helping.

46

UNIT 6 | Art (1)

Although specialized AI detection programs are still being developed and refined and often require specialized knowledge to operate, some are available and can assist in identifying AI-generated content. Fake or "doctored" images have a long history and have been around ever since humans started recording what they saw. Nowadays, however, it has become easier $_{25}$ for anyone to create or alter images so that they appear authentic. Though the majority of such enhanced images are for innocent personal diversion or for the purpose of enhancing creative products, the door has been opened to counterfeiting and the spread of false information. Now, more than ever, people need to maintain a state of healthy skepticism and continue to develop verification techniques in order to accurately differentiate between authentic and synthetic $_{30}$ images.

1. What is the main topic of this passage?
   (A) How to create realistic images
   (B) Distinguishing between real and AI-generated images
   (C) How to take good photographs
   (D) The history of AI image-enhancing technology

2. What do some websites and applications enable people to do?
   (A) Share real photos
   (B) Make fake images
   (C) Buy cameras
   (D) Learn computer science

3. The word "this" in line 9 refers to
   (A) the use of websites and applications
   (B) the growth of AI-generated images
   (C) the research by a university computer science professor
   (D) the challenge of identifying deep fakes

4. Why does the passage mention a university computer science professor?
   (A) To explain that people can spot fake photos
   (B) To say that learning about AI is hard
   (C) To show where to study photography
   (D) To tell us about a new university course

5. The word "counterfeit" in line 10 is closest in meaning
   (A) famous
   (B) pseudo
   (C) expensive
   (D) beautiful

**6.** What does the passage suggest about trusting our intuition?
   (A) It is not helpful.
   (B) It only works for experts and experienced users.
   (C) It is nothing compared to technology.
   (D) It is important when judging the authenticity of photos.

**7.** What should you look for in a photo to see if it has been made by AI?
   (A) Whether the resolution is fine or not
   (B) Elements like strange hand positions or light
   (C) When it was created
   (D) Whether it is color or black and white

**8.** What is the main point made in the last paragraph about fake photos?
   (A) They are becoming more common.
   (B) They have always been easy to make.
   (C) They have made it necessary to be more careful.
   (D) They are easier to spot now.

## Vocabulary Building (Section 3)

> このセクションに登場した単語を辞書で調べ，意味を書きましょう．また，調べた単語を使って，英文を完成させましょう．

(A) flaw          (n) _____          (D) diversion          (n) _____
(B) detection     (n) _____          (E) refine             (v) _____
(C) healthy       (adj) _____         (F) differentiate      (v) _____

**1.** Dogs are often used at airports for the _____ of illegal substances.
**2.** The artist fixed the _____ in the sculpture.
**3.** Video games are a popular form of _____, especially for younger people.

# UNIT 7

# Economics (1)

## 1. Listening Comprehension

このUnitではPart Bの形式を練習します．具体的には，学生どうしのやり取りを扱います．Warm upにも一部出ているように，会話中に各分野の専門用語が含まれる場合があります．一方，設問では必ずしも各分野の知識が問われるとは限りません．専門用語が出てきたとしても，慌てずに全体の流れを掴もうとする姿勢も大切です．ただ，用語を知っておくに越したことはありませんので，本書を通して分野の重要概念の一端を押さえておきましょう．

### Warm up

英語に対応する日本語を選びましょう．

1. elasticity　　　　（　）　　a. 厳しい
2. microeconomics　（　）　　b. ミクロ経済学
3. tough　　　　　（　）　　c. 対処する
4. handle　　　　　（　）　　d. 弾性

### Listening Exercises (1)  1-31〜33

Part Aと同じ形式の問題を解きましょう．このPartは，短い会話とそれに続く1つの質問から成ります．質問に対する最も適切な解答をそれぞれ (A)–(D) から選びましょう．

1. (A) She should enter the classroom as soon as possible.
   (B) She hasn't often sat in the front seat.
   (C) She thinks preparation for the class is important.
   (D) She is good at speaking in public.

2. (A) She is anxious about her job prospects.
   (B) She is confident that things will work out.
   (C) She feels pressured to make a decision.
   (D) She is indifferent to what interests the students.

3. (A) To look for an antidote in the forest
   (B) To call Professor Geller for advice
   (C) To wait and see if the swelling goes down
   (D) To take the woman to the hospital quickly

49

## Listening Exercises (2)  CD 1-34, 35

Part B と同じ形式の問題を解きましょう. この Part は, 長めの会話とそれに続く複数の質問から成ります.
質問に対する最も適切な解答をそれぞれ (A)–(D) から選びましょう.

1. (A) Inflation
   (B) Elasticity
   (C) Supply
   (D) Interest rates

2. (A) Reading the textbook carefully
   (B) Hiring an online tutor for help
   (C) Watching online materials
   (D) Asking their teacher for help

3. (A) Meet at the library
   (B) Call their professor
   (C) Take a break
   (D) Drop the course

4. (A) She has already watched them.
   (B) She didn't even think about watching them.
   (C) She is hesitant to watch them.
   (D) She does not think they are helpful.

## Vocabulary Building (Section 1)

> このセクションに登場した単語を辞書で調べ, 意味を書きましょう. また, 調べた単語を使って,
> 英文を完成させましょう.

(A) supply and demand curves
　　　　　　　　(n) ＿＿＿＿＿＿＿
(B) concept　　　(n) ＿＿＿＿＿＿＿
(C) overwhelmed　(adj) ＿＿＿＿＿＿

(D) tutorial　　　(n) ＿＿＿＿＿＿＿
(E) honestly　　　(adv) ＿＿＿＿＿＿＿
(F) cross one's mind　(v) ＿＿＿＿＿＿＿

1. I'm feeling ＿＿＿＿＿ by all the choices available.
2. I find it difficult to understand the abstract ＿＿＿＿＿ of elasticity.
3. Have you tried watching any online ＿＿＿＿＿ videos for the class?

50

UNIT 7 Economics (1)

# 2. Structure and Written Expression

知らない単語に出会ったときは，まず文脈から意味を推測してみましょう．前後の内容と単語の関係性を考えることで，ある程度の意味を推測できることがあります．その後，正しい意味を確認して覚えましょう．

## Warm up

英語に対応する日本語を選びましょう．

1. apprenticeship　　（　　）
2. affluent　　　　　（　　）
3. predecessor　　　（　　）
4. surge　　　　　　（　　）

a. 豊かな
b. 先人
c. 勃興
d. 見習い

## Structure Exercises

空欄に入る最も適切な語句を (A)–(D) から選び，英文を完成させましょう．

1. The original form of guilds first _____ during the 11th and 12th centuries, evolving from earlier trade associations.

   (A) admired
   (B) abandoned
   (C) emerged
   (D) skyrocketed

2. During the 10th and 11th centuries in Western Europe, there was a notable _____ in long-distance trade.

   (A) expansion
   (B) retention
   (C) supposition
   (D) radiation

3. When _____ the medieval feudal economic system, guilds are often mentioned as part of the broader urban economic structures.

   (A) in discussing
   (B) discussion
   (C) discussing
   (D) to discuss

4. Early merchant guilds comprised both merchants and a variety of craftsmen, but _____ evolved into specialized unions of similar craftsmen.

   (A) implicitly
   (B) eventually
   (C) fundamentally
   (D) precisely

51

5. Individuals established guilds to
   market their products at elevated prices
   and to support one another during
   difficult times, _____ over time, they
   increasingly exerted a significant
   impact on municipal politics.

   (A) already
   (B) yet
   (C) although
   (D) despite

6. In medieval Western society, there was
   a strict hierarchical system called the
   apprenticeship system in cities, and the
   masters at the top guided craftsmen
   and apprentices _____ in labor.

   (A) to engage
   (B) engagement
   (C) on engaging
   (D) for engaging

7. Florence is often described _____
   among the most affluent and
   prosperous cities in medieval Europe,
   renowned for its immense wealth and
   economic strength during that era.

   (A) to be
   (B) being
   (C) to have been
   (D) as having been

## Written Expression Exercises

英文中の誤った箇所を (A)–(D) から選びましょう.

1. The guilds in medieval London became the predecessors of corporations <u>responsibly</u> for
   <u>regulating</u> each profession, including training, <u>wage management</u>, <u>working conditions</u>,
   and industry standards.
   <br>(A: responsibly, B: regulating, C: wage management, D: working conditions)

2. In <u>the 14th and 15th centuries</u>, late medieval Europe experienced a surge in rural-to-
   urban migration of <u>the poor</u> and higher urban mortality rates, <u>fuel</u> by political unrest,
   wars, famine, epidemics, and shortages in trade and <u>essential supplies</u>.
   <br>(A: the 14th and 15th centuries, B: the poor, C: fuel, D: essential supplies)

3. The research <u>field</u> includes <u>studies</u> that explores various dimensions of guilds, <u>extends</u>
   beyond their traditional economic <u>roles and functions</u>.
   <br>(A: field, B: studies, C: extends, D: roles and functions)

UNIT 7 Economics (1)

4. In the medieval era, guilds predominantly existed in two forms: merchant guilds, which
                                                    A                                              B
   incorporated the majority of merchants within a specific town or city or craft guilds.
                  C                                                        D

5. Craft guilds appeared short after merchant guilds, originating in burgeoning towns where
                           A                              B
   a significant division of labor was becoming increasingly evident.
     C                              D

6. The rise of regulated companies and other associations of affluent merchant-capitalists
                A                              B
   gradually left the guilds increasingly detaching from the primary streams of economic
            C                              D
   influence.

7. In the Roman Empire, the government confined guild membership to hereditary artisans
   about skills passed down from generation to generation but increasing financial demands
   A                        B
   from the state resulted in the weakening of most guilds by the 4th century CE.
                   C                              D

## Vocabulary Building (Section 2)

> このセクションに登場した単語を辞書で調べ, 意味を書きましょう. また, 調べた単語を使って,
> 英文を完成させましょう.

(A) skyrocket     (v) _____     (D) radiation   (n) _____
(B) retention     (n) _____     (E) implicitly  (adv) _____
(C) supposition   (n) _____     (F) exert       (v) _____

1. The students demonstrated a model of a solar panel, and explained how it converts solar
   _____ into electricity.
2. Although she never explicitly said she was unhappy, her sighs and withdrawn demeanor
   _____ communicated her discontent.
3. The marathon runner needed to _____ every ounce of his energy in the final sprint.

53

# 3. Reading Comprehension

英文を読むスピードは words per minute (WPM) で測ることができます．パッセージの語数÷読み終わるのに要した時間（秒に換算）× 60 で算出できます．TOEFL Reading Section で必要な WPM は 150-200 と言われています．

## Warm up

英語に対応する日本語を選びましょう．

| | | | | |
|---|---|---|---|---|
| **1.** advent | ( ) | **a.** 支持者 |
| **2.** proponent | ( ) | **b.** 出現・到来 |
| **3.** address | ( ) | **c.** 統合する |
| **4.** enhance | ( ) | **d.** 高める |
| **5.** integrate | ( ) | **e.** 対処する |

## Reading Exercises

次の文章を読み，下の問いに対する最も適切な解答をそれぞれ (A)–(D) から選びましょう．

The hospitality industry has witnessed a remarkable innovation: the introduction of robot servers. These robot servers, often resembling a human child in size and adorned with charming, catlike features, are increasingly visible in restaurants worldwide. Their primary functions include greeting guests, leading them to their tables, returning dirty dishes, and

5　delivering food and beverages.

The advent of robot servers has sparked a debate about their role in the future of dining. Proponents argue that these robots can address labor shortages in the industry. For instance, a university official reported that when their campus restaurant employed robots, it noticeably enhanced service efficiency by reducing the workload on human staff. Globally, the

10　popularity of robot servers has surged, with tens of thousands now operating in various restaurants.

On the economic front, the introduction of robot servers has proven financially beneficial for some establishments. A restaurant reported that tasks previously managed by five or six employees are now efficiently handled by just three individuals, thanks to the robot

15　servers. This has led to significant cost savings, as the monthly expense of maintaining a robot is approximately one-third that of an employee's salary. Additionally, customers often share videos of these robotic servers on social media, indirectly boosting the restaurant's popularity.

However, not all experiences with robot servers have been positive. Critics point out that these machines cannot navigate stairs or take orders as humans do, which limits their

20　functionality. A business emphasized that restaurants are chaotic, which makes it challenging to integrate robots effectively. Furthermore, some establishments have found that robots hinder the efficiency of human servers due to their slow movement. Customer feedback also reflects mixed reactions; in a survey, about 60 percent of patrons felt that the robots did not enhance

UNIT 7 Economics (1)

their dining experience.

As the usage of robot servers expands, the question of whether robots can completely     25
replace human servers in the restaurant sector continues. While they have some advantages, it
is clear that they have limitations and issues that must be addressed. The future of robot
servers in the dining industry is unknown, with technological improvements playing a critical
part in deciding their function and effectiveness.

1.  What is the main point of the passage?
    (A) Technological improvements in robot design
    (B) The economic benefits of robot servers
    (C) The discussion of restaurant labor shortages
    (D) The effect of introducing robot servers in the hospitality business

2.  What is one of the essential duties of robot servers?
    (A) Bringing food and beverages to tables
    (B) Gathering client comments
    (C) Playing music in restaurants
    (D) Preparing meals in the kitchen

3.  What is the purpose of mentioning a report from a university official in the second
    paragraph?
    (A) To compare universities with restaurants
    (B) To criticize the usage of robots in educational settings
    (C) To demonstrate the educational benefits of robots
    (D) To provide an example of improved service efficiency

4.  The word "chaotic" in line 20 is closest in meaning to
    (A) disorganized
    (B) exciting
    (C) orderly
    (D) quiet

5.  The word "they" in line 26 refers to
    (A) Human servers
    (B) Robot servers
    (C) Restaurant owners
    (D) Technological advances

55

6. What may be inferred about restaurants that employ robot servers?
   (A) Human employees have been totally replaced by robots.
   (B) They are all quite profitable.
   (C) They are typically seen on college campuses.
   (D) They have difficulties in incorporating robots.

7. What is the limitation of robot servers?
   (A) They are prohibitively expensive to maintain.
   (B) They are unable to climb stairs.
   (C) They frequently fail.
   (D) They misunderstand commands.

8. What is the general conclusion from the passage about robot servers?
   (A) They are widely accepted and effective.
   (B) They are an occasional trend in the hotel business.
   (C) Their implementation brings benefits and obstacles.
   (D) They are less expensive than hiring human workers.

## Vocabulary Building (Section 3)

> このセクションに登場した単語を辞書で調べ, 意味を書きましょう. また, 調べた単語を使って, 英文を完成させましょう.

(A) hospitality (n) _____   (D) functionality (n) _____
(B) efficiency (n) _____   (E) hinder (v) _____
(C) front (n) _____

1. AI is a new _____ in business.
2. Good _____ attracts more customers to a restaurant.
3. Unexpected costs can _____ the growth of a small business.

# UNIT 8
## History (2)

### 1. Listening Comprehension

Listening Section ではイントネーションから得られる情報も内容を推測するのに役立つ場合があります．最初の話者が主張したことに対して，次の話者がどのようなイントネーションで応じたのか，強調したいのはどの点なのか，といった観点でイントネーションに着目してみると良いでしょう．会話ではイントネーションしだいで文字通りの意味とは異なるニュアンスが込められることもあるので，意識的に聞く必要があります．

### Warm up

英語に対応する日本語を選びましょう．

1. ethnoarchaeology    (　)     a. 解釈する
2. contemporary        (　)     b. 民族考古学
3. practice            (　)     c. 現代の
4. interpret           (　)     d. 習慣

### Listening Exercises (1)   1-36〜38

Part A と同じ形式の問題を解きましょう．この Part は，短い会話とそれに続く1つの質問から成ります．質問に対する最も適切な解答をそれぞれ (A)–(D) から選びましょう．

1. (A) They both agree that summer vacation is too short.
   (B) They differ on how vacation time should be allocated.
   (C) They both think that studying abroad is not a priority.
   (D) They agree that other breaks should be shortened to extend summer vacation.

2. (A) The course now requires a special textbook.
   (B) The course has been canceled due to low enrollment.
   (C) Students are now required to bring their own magnifying glasses.
   (D) The professor will provide magnifying glasses to the students.

3. (A) She will receive extra credit for the course.
   (B) She will meet the attendance requirement for the course.
   (C) She will have to attend additional classes.
   (D) She will be disqualified from future tournaments.

## Listening Exercises (2)  🎧 1-39, 40

Part C と同じ形式の問題を解きましょう. この Part は, 長めの講義・スピーチとそれに続く複数の質問から成ります. 質問に対する最も適切な解答をそれぞれ (A)–(D) から選びましょう.

1. (A) By predicting future trends in culture based on the experimental findings
   (B) By analyzing ancient texts and their author
   (C) By drawing parallels between contemporary and ancient societies
   (D) By examining historical works of art and their production methods

2. (A) Advanced dating technology
   (B) Comparative studies of present-day object usage
   (C) Restoration of old artifacts
   (D) Replicating methods used in archaeological discoveries

3. (A) Focus on diverse ethnic groups
   (B) Integration of various disciplines
   (C) Its status as an emerging field
   (D) Exclusive use of archaeological techniques

4. (A) Finding historical mysteries
   (B) Reading unreadable stories
   (C) Making complex machines
   (D) Creating artworks

## Vocabulary Building (Section 1)

このセクションに登場した単語を辞書で調べ, 意味を書きましょう. また, 調べた単語を使って, 英文を完成させましょう.

(A) artifact        (n) _____      (D) mystery       (n) _____
(B) reconstruction  (n) _____      (E) infer         (v) _____
(C) delve into      (v) _____      (F) educated      (adj) _____

1. We study contemporary societies to infer how specific ancient _____ was used.
2. I want to investigate the _____ of biological evolution on an island.
3. We can make a(n) _____ guess about past practices.

58

UNIT 8 | History (2)

## 2. Structure and Written Expression

複雑な文でも，主語，動詞，目的語，修飾語などの基本構造を見抜く練習をしましょう．正しい選択肢を選ぶには文の構造の理解が不可欠です．一文一文を正確に読めるようになることは，長文読解にとっても重要です．

### Warm up

英語に対応する日本語を選びましょう．

1. profit ( )    **a.** 利益
2. convection ( )    **b.** 移行する
3. explode ( )    **c.** 対流
4. transition ( )    **d.** 爆発する

### Structure Exercises

空欄に入る最も適切な語句を (A)–(D) から選び，英文を完成させましょう．

1. A lot of people hurried to California within a year _____ the initial discovery of gold.

   (A) following
   (B) subsequently
   (C) previous
   (D) initially

2. In the Mother Lode area of California's Sierra Nevada mountains, a large number of people started gold mining in one year, _____ to find a lot of gold and become rich.

   (A) hoped
   (B) hopes
   (C) hoping
   (D) were hoping

3. San Francisco, initially a small and sparsely _____ area, saw its population explode as a result of the Gold Rush.

   (A) populating
   (B) population
   (C) populated
   (D) populous

4. The Gold Rush did not yield profits for the majority; _____, substantial wealth was amassed by only an extremely limited number of individuals.

   (A) indeed
   (B) despite
   (C) furthermore
   (D) never

59

5. Geologists use the process of radiometric decay to find out the ages of Earth materials in years and to determine _____ geologic events like exhumation and subduction happened.

(A) that
(B) when
(C) what
(D) why

6. Since decay happens at a _____ rate, scientists can calculate a sample's age by measuring the decayed material and comparing it to the original amount.

(A) steady
(B) random
(C) variable
(D) unpredictable

7. Scientists use the term "half-lives" to describe how long it takes _____ 50 percent of a radioactive isotope's atoms to transition into a new isotope.

(A) to
(B) in
(C) as
(D) for

# Written Expression Exercises

英文中の誤った箇所を (A)–(D) から選びましょう.

1. Absolute dating <u>involves analyzing</u> the physical, chemical, and biological properties of
                  **A**
   materials, along with <u>historical association</u> like coins and <u>records with knowing dates,</u>
                          **B**                      **C**
   <u>to determine</u> the age of artifacts and buildings.
      **D**

2. Decay happens at a consistent rate, which allows scientists <u>to</u> measure the <u>decaying</u>
                                            **A**         **B**
   content in a sample, ascertain the proportion of original to material, <u>and</u> subsequently
                                                  **C**
   <u>estimate</u> the age of the sample.
     **D**

3. The <u>nucleus</u> of a radioactive atom undergoes <u>spontaneous</u> change to <u>becoming</u> a nucleus
        **A**                            **B**            **C**
   <u>of</u> a more stable, different isotope in radiometric decay.
   **D**

UNIT 8 History (2)

4. Geologists use radiometric decay to <u>date</u> Earth's materials and study <u>process</u> like the
   A B
   <u>uncovering</u> of rocks and the movement of tectonic plates beneath <u>others</u>.
   C D

5. <u>In contrast</u> the goldfields in North America and Australia that were typically <u>exhausted</u>
   A B
   after several years, the mining activities in Witwatersrand <u>have been expanding</u> since the
   C
   1890s, making <u>this region</u> one of the leading gold producers globally.
   D

6. The nature of South Africa's gold rush stood apart from <u>them</u> in North America and
   A
   Australia, <u>where</u>, in 1886, gold <u>was</u> unearthed in the Witwatersrand region of the
   B C
   Transvaal by a diamond miner <u>from</u> Kimberley, George Harrison.
   D

7. Australia's 1851 gold rush, <u>marked</u> by the discovery <u>of</u> rich deposits in Victoria's
   A B
   Ballarat and Bendigo areas, <u>drew</u> miners to Melbourne <u>across</u> Australia and England,
   C D
   with its peak lasting into the early 1860s.

## Vocabulary Building (Section 2)

このセクションに登場した単語を辞書で調べ, 意味を書きましょう. また, 調べた単語を使って,
英文を完成させましょう.

(A) stable (adj) _____ (D) indeed (adv) _____
(B) spontaneous (adj) _____ (E) unearth (v) _____
(C) sparsely (adv) _____ (F) decay (v) _____

1. The rural landscape was _____ populated, with houses scattered far apart across the
   rolling hills.
2. The wooden bench in the park had started to _____ due to years of exposure to rain
   and sun.
3. In response to the sudden change in market conditions, the company's board made a
   _____ decision to alter their investment strategy.

61

# 3. Reading Comprehension

英文は，文単位より句などのカタマリ（チャンク）ごとに理解する方がよいと言われています．チャンクは英文をスラッシュ (/) に切り，その次のスラッシュまでのおよそ 5 語 ± 2 語のカタマリを指します．これは人がパッと見て認識できる語数とも一致します．チャンクは前置詞，接続（関係）詞，to 不定詞，動詞の前で切ることが一般的です．

## Warm up

英語に対応する日本語を選びましょう．

1. employ      (     )      **a.** 加速する
2. accelerate  (     )      **b.** 絶え間ない
3. initiate    (     )      **c.** 始める
4. facet       (     )      **d.** 用いる
5. perpetual   (     )      **e.**（物事の）一面

## Reading Exercises

次の文章を読み，下の問いに対する最も適切な解答をそれぞれ (A)–(D) から選びましょう．

The inception of the Internet can be traced back to the Cold War era of the 1960s. During this period, the United States Department of Defense was actively seeking methods to fortify computer networks against potential threats, most notably nuclear war. As a consequence, ARPANET was developed employing a technique referred to as "packet

5　switching." This method is implemented by partitioning a message into smaller segments, which are then routed to their destination using the most efficient means possible. Introduced to the public for the first time in 1969, ARPANET emerged as a pivotal innovation, laying the foundation for the Internet as we know it today and fundamentally altering the manner in which research institutions exchanged information.

10　Internet expansion accelerated during the 1980s and 1990s. In 1989, Tim Berners-Lee introduced the World Wide Web (WWW), an Internet-based platform designed to streamline the process of retrieving information. This innovation initiated the migration of the Internet from research and academic environments to domestic settings. The proliferation of commercial Internet service providers by the mid-1990s stimulated a substantial surge in

15　Internet connectivity. During this time period, email, online forums, and web browsing were also widely adopted as indispensable components of daily life.

At present, the Internet connects more than four billion individuals worldwide, exerting influence on all facets of our society, economy, and cultural customs. The Internet's swift progression has been driven by the implementation of novel technologies, such as cloud

20　computing, social networks, and smartphones. These have significantly altered the ways in which we obtain information, engage in communication, and carry out commercial activities. With the incorporation of advanced Internet connected devices, virtual reality, and artificial intelligence, the Internet is anticipated to continue to develop and improve, ultimately enhancing connectivity and the quality of our experiences. The historical account of the Internet is not limited to technological progress; it also serves as a testament to the perpetual    25 pursuit of enhanced communication and endeavors of humanity to establish more intimate global connections.

1. What is the main idea of the passage?
   (A) The development and impact of the Internet
   (B) The history of the Cold War
   (C) The biography of Tim Berners-Lee
   (D) The role of smartphones in modern society

2. What was the original purpose of the ARPANET?
   (A) To provide a platform for social networking
   (B) To streamline searching for and retrieving information
   (C) To connect over four billion people worldwide
   (D) To protect computer networks in emergency situations

3. The word "pivotal" in line 7 is closest in meaning to
   (A) unnecessary
   (B) essential
   (C) temporary
   (D) outdated

4. Which of the following sentences has the same meaning as "The Internet's swift progression has been driven by the implementation of novel technologies" in lines 18-19?
   (A) The Internet has not changed much since its inception.
   (B) Introducing new technologies has accelerated the expansion of the Internet.
   (C) The Internet has led to the development of new technologies.
   (D) Introducing new technologies has hindered the growth of the Internet.

5. From the information in the passage, it can be inferred that the Internet
   (A) will stop developing in the near future.
   (B) has had little impact on our daily lives.
   (C) will continue to develop and affect many aspects of our lives.
   (D) was fully developed by the end of the 1960s.

6. The word "These" in line 20 refers to
   (A) four billion people worldwide.
   (B) all facets of our society, economy, and cultural practices.
   (C) new technologies such as cloud computing, social networking and smartphones.
   (D) advanced Internet connected devices, virtual reality, and artificial intelligence.

63

7. Which of the following sentences has the same meaning as "The historical account of the Internet is not limited to technological progress" in the third paragraph?
   (A) The history of the Internet includes additional elements beyond technological advances.
   (B) The history of the Internet only includes technological advances.
   (C) The history of the Internet does not include technological advances.
   (D) The history of the Internet is limited to the history of technology.

8. Based on the information in the passage, it can be inferred that the World Wide Web (WWW)
   (A) made the Internet less accessible to the public.
   (B) was introduced to limit the spread of the Internet.
   (C) made it easier to find and access information on the Internet.
   (D) was not a significant development in the history of the Internet.

## Vocabulary Building (Section 3)

このセクションに登場した単語を辞書で調べ，意味を書きましょう．また，調べた単語を使って，英文を完成させましょう．

(A) fortify      (v) _____      (D) indispensable      (adj) _____

(B) alter      (v) _____      (E) implementation      (n) _____

(C) proliferation      (n) _____

1. You need to _____ your password with some special characters.
2. Computers _____ how we work.
3. The _____ of apps makes life more convenient.

# UNIT 9

# Psychology (2)

## 1. Listening Comprehension

Listening Section の成績が思うように伸びない学習者は，どの点が苦手なのかを分析してみましょう．文法や語法は意識的に学ぶ学習者が多いですが，音声面でも意識的に学習可能なパターンは沢山あります．とりわけ，実際の発話では辞書通りに発音されない様々な現象が重要です．たとえば，機能語は曖昧な発音になる弱形をもち，前後の単語との関係では音声が連結・欠落したり，別の音が挿入されたりする場合もあります．

### Warm up

英語に対応する日本語を選びましょう．

1. workload       (　)       a. 治療
2. clinical       (　)       b. 仕事量
3. therapy        (　)       c. 包括的な
4. comprehensive  (　)       d. 臨床の

### Listening Exercises (1)    1-41〜43

Part A と同じ形式の問題を解きましょう．この Part は，短い会話とそれに続く1つの質問から成ります．質問に対する最も適切な解答をそれぞれ (A)–(D) から選びましょう．

1. (A) Some historical documents
   (B) Feedback on other students' presentation
   (C) A term paper about archaic language
   (D) A book about a code of conduct

2. (A) The woman speaks in support of history
   (B) The woman is overwhelmed by how much she has to learn
   (C) The man does not understand what the woman wants to say
   (D) They both are negative about studying history

3. (A) Preserving ancient records using electronic devices
   (B) Reading primary sources all by themselves
   (C) Understanding the historical contexts of ancient crafts
   (D) Exploring some ancient tools in a cave

## Listening Exercises (2)　🎧 1-44, 45

Part B と同じ形式の問題を解きましょう. この Part は, 長めの会話とそれに続く複数の質問から成ります.
質問に対する最も適切な解答をそれぞれ (A)–(D) から選びましょう.

**1.** (A) The difficulty of the subject itself
　　(B) Dealing with the workload
　　(C) The location of the university
　　(D) The reputation of the graduate school

**2.** (A) As a hard-to-tolerate experience
　　(B) As challenging but intellectually satisfying
　　(C) As undoubtedly beneficial for a career path
　　(D) As focused only on academic research

**3.** (A) Educational psychology
　　(B) Developmental psychology
　　(C) Industrial-organizational psychology
　　(D) Children's psychology

**4.** (A) Taking out a loan from the university
　　(B) Applying for scholarships and seeking part-time work
　　(C) Focusing on his/her studies
　　(D) Choosing a more affordable program offered by the universiy

## Vocabulary Building (Section 1)

> このセクションに登場した単語を辞書で調べ, 意味を書きましょう. また, 調べた単語を使って,
> 英文を完成させましょう.

(A) hesitant　　(adj) ＿＿＿＿＿＿　　(D) debate　　(v) ＿＿＿＿＿＿

(B) intellectually　(adv) ＿＿＿＿＿＿　(E) potentially　(adv) ＿＿＿＿＿＿

(C) satisfying　(adj) ＿＿＿＿＿＿　　(F) tuition　　(n) ＿＿＿＿＿＿

**1.** What specific aspects of the offer are making you ＿＿＿＿ to accept it?

**2.** You would ＿＿＿＿ between the two job offers, as they both have their pros and cons.

**3.** I have to pay the ＿＿＿＿ by myself.

UNIT 9 Psychology (2)

## 2. Structure and Written Expression

前置詞や接続詞の基本的な知識を整理しておきましょう. 例えば, because と because of の使い分けなどです. 用例を確認し, 正しい使い方を身につけてください.

### Warm up

英語に対応する日本語を選びましょう.

1. sphere          (  )          **a.** 分野
2. phenomenon   (  )          **b.** 深い
3. scholarly      (  )          **c.** 学術的な
4. profound       (  )          **d.** 現象

### Structure Exercises

空欄に入る最も適切な語句を (A)–(D) から選び, 英文を完成させましょう.

1. For Freud, the field of art was _____ significance in the sphere of humanities.

   (A) in
   (B) to
   (C) for
   (D) of

2. In the 1890s, Freud collaborated with Austrian physician and physiologist Josef Breuer, studying neurotic _____ under hypnosis.

   (A) patients
   (B) patient
   (C) patiently
   (D) patience

3. The term "psychoanalysis" might sound like it _____ strictly to the fields of psychology or medicine, yet its strong connection to the humanities is not as commonly recognized.

   (A) belongs
   (B) attracts
   (C) attends
   (D) believes

4. Ambivalence refers to the mental phenomenon _____ one directs conflicting emotions or attitudes, such as love and hatred, toward the same object.

   (A) how
   (B) where
   (C) which
   (D) what

67

**5.** "Hysteria" was commonly used to describe a state of uncontrollable and _____ emotions and can denote a transient mental or emotional condition.

(A) excessive
(B) extensive
(C) expansive
(D) expensive

**6.** As a form of depth psychology, psychoanalysis explores mental life from three perspectives: dynamic, economic, and _____.

(A) topographies
(B) topographically
(C) topography
(D) topographical

**7.** Freud's early years were spent in Vienna, where he attended school and university, got married, trained as both a researcher and a doctor, and _____ developing the field of psychoanalysis.

(A) has begun
(B) begin
(C) had begun
(D) began

## Written Expression Exercises

英文中の誤った箇所を (A)–(D) から選びましょう.

**1.** Sigmund Freud <u>founded</u> psychoanalysis in Vienna <u>at the start</u> of the 20th century,
　　　　　　　　　**A**　　　　　　　　　　　　　　　　**B**
building it upon the concept <u>of</u> the human mind consists of <u>both</u> conscious and
　　　　　　　　　　　　　**C**　　　　　　　　　　　　　　　**D**
unconscious aspects.

**2.** Although Adler, <u>was famous</u> for Adlerian psychology, <u>initially</u> shared a close relationship
　　　　　　　　　**A**　　　　　　　　　　　　　　　　**B**
with Freud, their <u>scholarly</u> assertions <u>eventually</u> took different paths.
　　　　　　　　**C**　　　　　　　**D**

**3.** <u>In contrast</u> emotions like, anger, sorrow, and pleasure often manifest <u>explosively</u> and are
　　**A**　　　　　　　　　　　　　　　　　　　　　　　　　　**B**
short-lived, <u>feelings of worry and anxiety</u> tend to be more restrained, <u>yet</u> they persist for
　　　　　**C**　　　　　　　　　　　　　　　　　　　　**D**
longer periods.

UNIT 9 Psychology (2)

4. <u>Through</u> urging the patient to share any spontaneous thoughts that arose through
     **A**
   association, free association aimed to unveil <u>previous</u> unspoken aspects of the psyche,
     **B**
   which Freud, in a <u>long-standing</u> tradition, referred to as the <u>unconscious</u>.
     **C**  **D**

5. Freud's research <u>on</u> hysteria <u>included</u> an exploration of female sexuality and <u>her</u> potential
     **A**  **B**  **C**
   to manifest in neurotic <u>ways</u>.
     **D**

6. It is difficult to identify specific causes <u>for</u> nervous disorders; whether a conflict results
     **A**
   in a healthy resolution <u>or</u> leads to a neurotic impairment of function <u>depend</u> on
     **B**  **C**
   quantitative factors, or the <u>relative</u> strength of the involved forces.
     **D**

7. Freud contended that unconscious motivations, <u>largely</u> stemming from <u>childhood</u>
     **A**  **B**
   experiences and complicated emotional responses to <u>parents and siblings</u>, predominantly
     **C**
   influence <u>humanity</u> behavior.
     **D**

## Vocabulary Building (Section 2)

---

このセクションに登場した単語を辞書で調べ, 意味を書きましょう. また, 調べた単語を使って,
英文を完成させましょう.

---

(A) unconscious  (adj) _____  (D) predominantly  (adv) _____
(B) manifest  (v) _____  (E) assertion  (n) _____
(C) impairment  (n) _____  (F) unveil  (v) _____

1. The lawyer decided to make an _____ that her client was innocent of the charges.
2. The museum is set to _____ its new exhibit next Saturday.
3. The population of the village is _____ agricultural, with most residents engaged in
   farming and related activities.

69

# 3. Reading Comprehension

文をスラッシュ (/) で区切ってチャンクをつくることのメリットはいくつかあり，1）文の構造が分かりやすくなる，2）語順通り読むことが容易になりスピードが上がる，3）リスニング力向上にもつながる，といったものです．

## Warm up

英語に対応する日本語を選びましょう．

1. utmost     ( )     **a.** 運命
2. inferiority     ( )     **b.** 枝分かれする
3. diverge     ( )     **c.** 最大限の
4. instinct     ( )     **d.** 本能
5. destiny     ( )     **e.** 劣っていること

## Reading Exercises

次の文章を読み，下の問いに対する最も適切な解答をそれぞれ (A)–(D) から選びましょう．

Adlerian psychology, which was developed by Alfred Adler, provides a unique perspective on the thoughts, emotions, and behaviors of humans. Adler believed that belonging to and having a sense of community were of utmost importance. He held the belief that all individuals begin life with a sense of inferiority and strive to overcome that sensation
5 throughout their lives. This desire to develop, according to Adler, is not egotistical. He viewed it as an opportunity for individuals to effect positive change in the world. He proposed that overcoming sentiments of inadequacy contributes to personal development. This development not only benefits us personally but also enables us to contribute positively to society. Strong emphasis is placed on encouraging and supporting one another in Adlerian psychology; this,
10 according to Adler, would result in an improved world for all.

Jungian psychology, which was first proposed by Carl Jung, diverges from the principles of Adler. The collective unconscious, as described by Jung, is comparable to a shared mental space that contains recollections and concepts from our predecessors. Archetypes, or common symbols, he believed, exert an influence on our behavior and
15 personalities on behalf of the collective unconscious. In contrast to Adler, who was concerned with conscious thought and social interaction, Jung emphasized the influence of unseen aspects of the mind on our thoughts and actions. Unlike Jungian psychology, Adlerian psychology posits that our decisions and objectives exert a greater influence on our actions than do these concealed forces.

20 Additionally, Freudian psychology, which was created by Sigmund Freud, is diametrically opposed to Adlerian psychology. Freud was preoccupied with the way in which our formative years are influenced by our early experiences, particularly our primal instincts and anxieties. He discussed the id, ego, and superego, which are frequently at odds with one

70

another as components of the human psyche. In contrast, Adler emphasized the significance of personal decisions and social factors in relation to these internal conflicts. He proposed a more 25 optimistic perspective on human nature and argued that we can shape our own destinies through mutual support and deliberate choice. Adlerian psychology is characterized by its positive perspective, which emphasizes the notion that despite being constrained by our past or aspirations, we have the ability to shape our own destinies.

1. Which of the following best describes the main idea of the passage?
   (A) Adlerian psychology emphasizes the importance of community and social interaction.
   (B) Adlerian psychology highlights the role of unconscious forces in shaping our personalities.
   (C) Adlerian psychology is diametrically opposed to Freudian psychology.
   (D) Adlerian psychology provides a further developed theory based on the ideas of Freud and Jung.

2. What does Adlerian psychology emphasize in its approach to human development?
   (A) The influence of early childhood experiences
   (B) The role of unconscious desires and conflicts
   (C) Personal growth facilitated by conquering feelings of inadequacy
   (D) The impact of past traumas and aspirations

3. The word "inferiority" in line 4 is closest in meaning to
   (A) A sense of inadequacy or lack of worth
   (B) A feeling that one is better or more important
   (C) A fear of failure and rejection
   (D) A belief in one's own abilities and potential

4. The word "it" in line 6 refers to
   (A) Belonging to a community
   (B) Having a sense of community
   (C) The desire to develop
   (D) The belief in the importance of community

5. What is the author's primary purpose in writing this passage?
   (A) To emphasize the similarities among Adlerian, Jungian, and Freudian psychologies
   (B) To criticize Adlerian psychology for its emphasis on social factors
   (C) To provide a chronological overview of Adler's life and his psychology
   (D) To argue that Adlerian psychology offers a more optimistic view of human nature

**6.** Which of the following sentences best expresses the main idea of the third paragraph?
(A) Freudian psychology emphasizes the role of the collective unconscious in shaping our personalities.
(B) Freudian psychology focuses on the importance of early childhood experiences in determining our future behavior.
(C) Freudian psychology views the desire for development as an opportunity for positive change in the world.
(D) Freudian psychology highlights the significance of personal decisions and social factors in shaping our destinies.

**7.** Jungian psychology differs from Adlerian psychology in that Carl Jung emphasizes
(A) the role of personal choices in shaping one's destiny.
(B) the importance of social interaction in individual development.
(C) the influence of the collective unconscious and archetypes on behavior and personality.
(D) the importance of overcoming feelings of inadequacy in personal development.

**8.** What is the tone of the passage?
(A) Objective and neutral
(B) Critical and skeptical
(C) Enthusiastic and supportive
(D) Argumentative and persuasive

## *Vocabulary Building* (Section 3)

> このセクションに登場した単語を辞書で調べ、意味を書きましょう。また、調べた単語を使って、英文を完成させましょう。

(A) community (n) _____  (D) at odds with (prep) _____
(B) egotistical (adj) _____  (E) in relation to (prep) _____
(C) on behalf of (prep) _____

**1.** According to some psychologists, a strong _____ can help people feel supported and less stressed.

**2.** Her radical ideas about happiness are _____ traditional psychological theories.

**3.** _____ our study group, I presented our findings on stress management techniques.

# UNIT 10
# Environment (2)

## 1. Listening Comprehension

Part B でも全体の主旨を理解することは重要です．設問では，主旨を直接問う形式のほか，全体を踏まえて次の行動を推論させる形式で理解が問われます．この Unit では，まずは話者どうしの関係性，会話の目的，会話が行われている場面を最初の 2−3 くらいの発話から理解することを目標の 1 つにしてみましょう．できる限り早い段階で会話の方向性をつかむことで，全体の主旨を理解しやすくなるはずです．

### Warm up

英語に対応する日本語を選びましょう．

| | | |
|---|---|---|
| 1. desertification | (　) | a. 砂漠化 |
| 2. revisit | (　) | b. 安心させる |
| 3. citation | (　) | c. 再検討する |
| 4. relieve | (　) | d. 引用 |

### Listening Exercises (1)  2-01〜03

Part A と同じ形式の問題を解きましょう．この Part は，短い会話とそれに続く 1 つの質問から成ります．質問に対する最も適切な解答をそれぞれ (A)–(D) から選びましょう．

1. (A) They make hormones work better.
   (B) They are chemicals that affect hormone functions.
   (C) They help the body produce more hormones.
   (D) They are a type of hormone.

2. (A) Methods of recycling plastic
   (B) The impact of plastic production
   (C) The issue of ocean pollution caused by the mass production
   (D) Developing sustainable alternatives to plastic

3. (A) The excessive costs of implementing green technology
   (B) The dilemma between economic growth and environmental protection
   (C) The role that wealthier people play in finding sustainable practices
   (D) The need to establish international organizations for sustainable development

73

### Listening Exercises (2)  🎧 2-04, 05

Part B と同じ形式の問題を解きましょう. この Part は, 長めの会話とそれに続く複数の質問から成ります.
質問に対する最も適切な解答をそれぞれ (A)–(D) から選びましょう.

1. (A) At the library's reference desk
   (B) In a classroom where environmental studies are being taught
   (C) In an architecture professor's office
   (D) At an exhibition on architectural technology

2. (A) Finding the section for architecture-related books
   (B) Understanding the content of the professor's handout
   (C) Finding books about desertification
   (D) Knowing how to use the library's search system

3. (A) The author's name
   (B) The year the book was published
   (C) The publisher's name
   (D) The genre the book belongs to

4. (A) To the architecture section
   (B) To the environmental studies section
   (C) To the new releases section
   (D) To the professor's office

### Vocabulary Building (Section 1)

このセクションに登場した単語を辞書で調べ, 意味を書きましょう. また, 調べた単語を使って, 英文を完成させましょう.

(A) unattended   (adj) _____   (D) inquiry    (n) _____
(B) locatable    (adj) _____   (E) landfill   (n) _____
(C) readily      (adv) _____   (F) librarian  (n) _____

1. The professor seems to have provided proper citations, so they should be easily _____.
2. Although my _____ isn't very complex, I would appreciate an explanation.
3. Plans to create a _____ should be abandoned due to environmental concerns.

74

UNIT 10 Environment (2)

## 2. Structure and Written Expression

単語の意味だけでなく，同義語や反意語も覚えることで，語彙の幅が広がります．類義語辞典を活用して，表現のバリエーションを増やしましょう．また，単語のニュアンスや使用場面を理解することで，英文の緻密な理解が可能になります．

### Warm up

英語に対応する日本語を選びましょう．

1. boundary      ( )     **a.** 大陸の
2. continental    ( )     **b.** 古生物学
3. paleontology   ( )     **c.** 密な
4. dense        ( )     **d.** 境界

### Structure Exercises

空欄に入る最も適切な語句を (A)–(D) から選び，英文を完成させましょう．

1. The lithosphere-asthenosphere boundary _____ as a detachment zone, allowing plate movement.

    (A) assigns
    (B) establishes
    (C) separates
    (D) functions

2. The lithosphere _____ of seven large continental and oceanic plates, six or seven medium-sized regional plates, and several smaller ones.

    (A) consists
    (B) removes
    (C) regards
    (D) makes

3. Following the proposal of the concept of continental drift, the theory of plate tectonics was _____.

    (A) developed
    (B) abbreviated
    (C) correlated
    (D) distinguished

4. In the early history of paleontology continents were believed _____ by land bridges or now-extinct continents.

    (A) to be connected
    (B) to connect
    (C) connecting
    (D) that they connect

75

5. _____ retrospection of Earth's geological past, it becomes clear that there were several occasions when continental glaciers expanded significantly across the globe.

(A) In
(B) To
(C) For
(D) Beyond

6. The geologist Arthur Holmes was the pioneering individual who proposed the concept of mantle convection _____ beneath the Earth's surface.

(A) that occur
(B) occurs
(C) occurring
(D) to have occurred

7. In the 1980s, the advancement in computer technology _____ researchers to examine seismic wave data from a variety of perspectives.

(A) let
(B) enabled
(C) made
(D) proposed

## Written Expression Exercises

英文中の誤った箇所を (A)–(D) から選びましょう.

1. The supercontinent which all continents were connected was named Pangaea, and the
                  **A**                  **B**                **C**
   splitting is thought to have begun in the Mesozoic era.
   **D**

2. The theory of continental drift suggests that the lighter continents float on a denser, fluid-
                           **A**                          **B**
   like layer of rocks, with mantle convection drive the movement of these continents.
               **C**                 **D**

3. One of the bases for Wegener's continental drift theory was the similarity of coastlines
     **A**                                    **B**
   and continuous geological structures on both side of South America and Africa.
              **C**                 **D**

4. There exist two divergent types of crust within the Earth's structure: the continental and
      **A**                          **B**
   the oceanic, each of them exhibits unique differences in terms of their composition and
               **C**  **D**
   thickness.

UNIT 10 Environment (2)

5. The <u>varied</u> densities of lithospheric rocks <u>are reflected in</u> the <u>contrast</u> <u>average</u> heights of
      A                                                 B            C     D
   the continental and oceanic crusts.

6. During the <u>late</u> 20th and early 21st centuries, the understanding deepened <u>that</u> plate
             A                                                         B
   tectonics played a significant role <u>in shaping</u> Earth's atmosphere, oceans, climate, and
                                           C
   the <u>evolution</u> environment for life.
        D

7. In 1915, Wegener introduced a hypothesis <u>asserting</u> that Earth's continents, <u>once was a</u>
                                           A                                  B
   singular landmass, <u>have</u> since drifted apart to their <u>current</u> positions.
                     C                                    D

## *Vocabulary Building* (Section 2)

このセクションに登場した単語を辞書で調べ, 意味を書きましょう. また, 調べた単語を使って, 英文を完成させましょう.

(A) proposal      (n) _____      (D) split      (v) _____
(B) hypothesis    (n) _____      (E) continent   (n) _____
(C) retrospection  (n) _____      (F) drift      (v) _____

1. The scientist formulated a _____ that the new drug could significantly reduce the recovery time for patients.
2. After losing power, the ship began to _____ aimlessly in the open sea.
3. During the meeting, opinions were _____; half of the members supported the proposal, while the other half opposed it.

# 3. Reading Comprehension

設問を解くには，まず質問文に目を通しておくことが重要です．特に本文中の情報を探す問題では，質問文にあるキーワードを見つけ，それが出てくる場所を特定しておけば，その箇所に解答の根拠があります．

## Warm up

英語に対応する日本語を選びましょう．

1. cornerstone （　）　　**a.** 基礎
2. substantial （　）　　**b.** 妨げる
3. hinder （　）　　**c.** 実施
4. anticipate （　）　　**d.** 相当な
5. implementation （　）　　**e.** 予想する

## Reading Exercises

次の文章を読み，下の問いに対する最も適切な解答をそれぞれ (A)–(D) から選びましょう．

　　An unmistakable worldwide shift is occurring towards a more ecologically aware and sustainable future, with renewable energy sources taking the lead. The global energy sector has traditionally depended significantly on fossil fuels, which have served as the cornerstone of energy production and economic progress. The significant environmental damage and

5　impact of obtaining and burning fossil fuels have led to a worldwide reevaluation and planned transition toward renewable energy sources. Technological advancements in hydropower, wind power, and photovoltaic (PV) systems have driven a paradigm shift, lowering global reliance on fossil fuels and aiding in the battle against climate change.

　　Renewable energy is seeing fast growth, with solar panels and wind turbines becoming

10　more prevalent globally. The rise in renewable energy adoption is driven by substantial investments from public and private sectors that acknowledge the significance of clean energy technology in attaining environmental sustainability and energy security. Although progress is positive, the shift to a completely renewable energy system is hindered by various obstacles. Key challenges in maximizing the utilization of renewable resources include energy storage,

15　grid integration, and guaranteeing the economic sustainability of renewable energy projects.

　　The future prospects for renewable energy are highly promising. Continual technical advancements are anticipated to enhance the effectiveness and dependability of renewable energy sources. The integration of smart grids and distributed energy systems has the capacity to revolutionize the energy sector by enhancing energy distribution, minimizing waste, and

20　enhancing the reliability and efficiency of energy systems. Emerging technologies such as hydrogen fuel cells and wave energy converters are expected to revolutionize the energy sector by offering creative answers to current energy issues. An environmentally sustainable energy landscape can be achieved by investing in research and development, making financial commitments, and implementing progressive policies to enable universal access to clean, affordable, and equitable energy.

Ultimately, the worldwide implementation of renewable energy is crucial for securing a sustainable and thriving future. Our current decisions will significantly and enduringly affect future generations. By dedicating ourselves to developing and incorporating renewable energy sources, we support both economic growth and environmental preservation. This commitment supports a healthier and more sustainable future by strengthening our collective duty to conserve our earth for future generations.

1. What is the main purpose of the passage?
   (A) To list the issues associated with the use of fossil fuels
   (B) To detail renewable energy advancements and cost reductions
   (C) To compare renewable energy sources with fossil fuels
   (D) To discuss the shift towards renewable energy and its significance

2. What has been a cornerstone of energy production and economic progress?
   (A) Hydrogen fuel cells
   (B) Distributed energy systems
   (C) Fossil fuels
   (D) Wind power

3. What is a significant consequence of obtaining and burning fossil fuels mentioned in the passage?
   (A) Increased economic sustainability
   (B) Enhanced energy distribution
   (C) Significant environmental damage
   (D) Improved energy security

4. What term does the passage use to describe the global movement towards more sustainable energy solutions?
   (A) Economic revolution
   (B) Paradigm shift
   (C) Technological transition
   (D) Environmental reevaluation

5. The passage mentions "smart grids." What is implied about their role in the future of energy?
   (A) They will limit the growth of renewable energy sources.
   (B) They will attract investors exclusively in developing nations.
   (C) They will make energy sources infinite.
   (D) They will increase the reliability of traditional energy systems.

**6.** Which of the following best represents the phrase "driven by substantial investments from public and private sectors" in lines 10-11?

(A) Led by significant financial support from government and business

(B) Pushed forward by the public and private sector's cautious approach

(C) Moved by the private sector's resistance to change

(D) Hindered by the public sector's lack of funding

**7.** What does the term "economic sustainability" in line 15 refer to in the context of renewable energy projects?

(A) The ability to produce energy without financial support

(B) Ensuring the long-term profitability of projects

(C) The impact of renewable energy on global economics

(D) Reducing the cost of renewable energy to below that of fossil fuels

**8.** How does the passage suggest we can achieve an environmentally sustainable energy landscape?

(A) By ceasing all investment in fossil fuels immediately

(B) Through research, financial commitment, and progressive policies

(C) By fully relying on current technologies without further innovation

(D) Through government regulation of the energy sector only

## Vocabulary Building (Section 3)

> このセクションに登場した単語を辞書で調べ, 意味を書きましょう. また, 調べた単語を使って, 英文を完成させましょう.

(A) obtain (v) _____

(B) reevaluation (n) _____

(C) acknowledge (v) _____

(D) guarantee (v) _____

(E) crucial (adj) _____

**1.** The transition to renewable energy is _____ for the future of the planet.

**2.** There is no way to _____ the success of any renewable energy project.

**3.** There has been a(n) _____ of the role of fossil fuels in the wake of climate change.

# UNIT 11

# Science and Technology (2)

## 1. Listening Comprehension

この Unit では Part C の講義形式の発話を扱います．専門用語は，ギリシア語やラテン語に由来するものが多く，多音節で聞き取りにくい場合も少なくありません．そのような語に関して，背景知識は前提とされませんが，その用語に関連する設問が出される場合があります．はっきりと聞き取れなかった場合や，聞き取れてもスペルが分からない場合でも，諦めずに何らかのメモを残しておき，周辺の語や表現から推測していきましょう．

### Warm up

英語に対応する日本語を選びましょう．

1. devoid     (   )   a. 広々とした
2. spacious   (   )   b. 〜を辿る
3. genesis    (   )   c. 起源
4. trace      (   )   d. 欠如している

### Listening Exercises (1)  2-06〜08

Part A と同じ形式の問題を解きましょう．この Part は，短い会話とそれに続く 1 つの質問から成ります．質問に対する最も適切な解答をそれぞれ (A)–(D) から選びましょう．

1. (A) The technical difficulties of using old cameras
   (B) The uniqueness of film photography
   (C) The cost of buying and maintaining old cameras
   (D) The superiority of old cameras over digital ones

2. (A) The difficulty of taking black-and-white photos
   (B) The emotional depth of black-and-white photos
   (C) The popularity of black-and-white photos on social media
   (D) The technical aspects of black-and-white film development

3. (A) Daguerre's career as a professional photographer
   (B) Daguerre's invention of the daguerreotype
   (C) Daguerre's contributions to painting techniques
   (D) The financial success of Daguerre's photography business

### Listening Exercises (2)　CD 2-09, 10

Part C と同じ形式の問題を解きましょう．この Part は，長めの講義・スピーチとそれに続く複数の質問から成ります．質問に対する最も適切な解答をそれぞれ (A)–(D) から選びましょう．

1. (A) Small device
   (B) Small chamber
   (C) Handheld gadget
   (D) Artistic tool

2. (A) Ancient Greece
   (B) The early modern period
   (C) Medieval
   (D) Industrial Revolution

3. (A) To create precise drawings
   (B) To capture family portraits
   (C) To experiment with light
   (D) To develop photographs

4. (A) He developed the camera.
   (B) He taught artists and painters how to use the camera.
   (C) He discovered the principles of the camera obscura.
   (D) He took the first photograph using a camera.

### Vocabulary Building (Section 1)

> このセクションに登場した単語を辞書で調べ，意味を書きましょう．また，調べた単語を使って，英文を完成させましょう．

| | | | | | |
|---|---|---|---|---|---|
| (A) | fascinating | (adj) _____ | (D) | embrace | (v) _____ |
| (B) | handheld | (adj) _____ | (E) | capture | (v) _____ |
| (C) | chamber | (n) _____ | (F) | intriguing | (adj) _____ |

1. Some painters in the era would _____ the camera obscura.
2. The Latin expression meaning "small _____" is thought to be the origin of the word "camera."
3. The _____ features of the device improve the portability of the original model.

82

UNIT 11 | Science and Technology (2)

## 2. Structure and Written Expression

リスニングにも積極的に取り組みましょう. Section 2 と関係ないように思えるかもしれませんがリスニングを通じてたくさんインプットすることで,「なんとなくこっちの方が自然」と思えるような語感が身についてきます.

### Warm up

英語に対応する日本語を選びましょう.

1. witness　　　　　（　）　　a. 目撃する
2. instrument　　　（　）　　b. 予備的な
3. preliminary　　　（　）　　c. 器械
4. landscape　　　　（　）　　d. 風景

### Structure Exercises

空欄に入る最も適切な語句を (A)–(D) から選び, 英文を完成させましょう.

1. Significant technological advancements in the history of the camera obscura were _____ during the 16th century.

    (A) derived
    (B) regarded
    (C) disposed
    (D) witnessed

2. A pinhole camera creates images by capturing light that enters through a small hole, _____ using a lens, to expose the film.

    (A) despite
    (B) instead of
    (C) regardless
    (D) although

3. The camera obscura, which laid the groundwork for today's cameras, was _____ a useful tool for astronomers.

    (A) older
    (B) once
    (C) former
    (D) previous

4. The early camera obscuras, often _____, were either entire darkened rooms or large tents, unlike their smaller modern counterparts.

    (A) was vast
    (B) vastly
    (C) vast
    (D) vastness

83

5. The original camera lucida, often hard to focus, was improved _____ adding a weak spectacle lens between the prism and the paper.

(A) in
(B) by
(C) on
(D) to

6. None of Daguerre's microscopic or telescopic daguerreotypes survived because a fire in 1839 destroyed his laboratory, _____ his records and early experiments.

(A) along with
(B) because of
(C) for the sake of
(D) in accordance with

7. A camera obscura is a darkened room with a small hole in one wall that allows light to enter, projecting an inverted image of the outside world _____ the opposite wall.

(A) for
(B) onto
(C) with
(D) behind

## Written Expression Exercises

英文中の誤った箇所を (A)–(D) から選びましょう.

1. Some scholars suggest that the high interest in landscape painting contributed for the
   A                                                                          B
   increased popularity of the camera obscura around the 19th century.
   C                                                    D

2. Like many other artists on his time, Daguerre made preliminary sketches by tracing the
   A                      B                                                    C
   images produced by both the camera obscura and the camera lucida, a prism-fitted
   instrument that was invented in 1807.
              D

3. For centuries the technique was used for viewing eclipses of the Sun without endangering
   A                                    B                                        C
   the eyes and, by the 16th century, in an aid to drawing.
                                       D

4. The camera lucida uses a prism mounted above paper, enabling observers see a reflected
   A                                enabling              C
                                                         B
   image of an object on the paper when they position their eye near the prism's edge.
                                                D

84

**UNIT 11** Science and Technology (2)

5. Daguerre's interest <u>was in</u> shortening the exposure time <u>necessary</u> to obtain an image of
   the real world, <u>on the other hand</u> Niépce remained interested <u>in producing</u> reproducible
   plate.

   A     B     C     D

6. The camera obscura, <u>Latin for</u> "dark chamber," <u>originally</u> was a dark room with light
   <u>enter</u> through a tiny hole, and this equipment <u>existed</u> since ancient times.

   A     B     C     D

7. William Hyde Wollaston, <u>in a span of</u> three years, patented a new spectacle lens design
   in 1804, <u>followed by</u> the camera lucida in 1806, <u>and then</u> published a <u>detail</u> book on the
   camera lucida's design in 1807.

   A     B     C     D

## Vocabulary Building (Section 2)

> このセクションに登場した単語を辞書で調べ，意味を書きましょう．また，調べた単語を使って，
> 英文を完成させましょう．

(A) derive    (v) _____      (D) trace     (v) _____

(B) despite    (prep) _____      (E) popularity    (n) _____

(C) vast    (adj) _____      (F) contribute to    (v) _____

1. Many English words _____ their meaning from Latin roots.
2. Due to its health benefits, yoga has gained immense _____ in recent years.
3. He had a _____ collection of stamps from all over the world.

85

# 3. Reading Comprehension

設問を解く際の読み方は必ずしも同じではありません．全体の概要を理解するならば速読することが良いですが，情報を探し出す問題は，ヒントになる箇所を見つけたらその場所を少し落ち着いて読む必要あります．時間がないからと焦って読むとここで間違えます．

## Warm up

英語に対応する日本語を選びましょう．

1. significant （　） **a.** 構成要素
2. generation （　） **b.** 生成
3. contextually （　） **c.** 大きな
4. indicate （　） **d.** 示す
5. component （　） **e.** 文脈的に

## Reading Exercises

次の文章を読み，下の問いに対する最も適切な解答をそれぞれ (A)−(D) から選びましょう．

Language processing tasks, such as text generation and machine translation have made significant progress with the development of Artificial Intelligence (AI). With large datasets, AI can generate contextually appropriate responses that sometimes appear human-like. This capability might indicate that AI shows human-like intelligence and understanding. Still, the

5 data-driven processing of AI is fundamentally different from human cognition.

AI is constrained by the data produced by humans: it cannot create language on its own. Unlike AI, humans learn languages autonomously by associating words with real-life experiences. This approach is clearly different from that of AI, which relies on identifying patterns in large datasets. For example, infants acquire the word "dog" from sensory

10 experiences such as seeing it, hearing its bark, touching and interacting with it. Later, when they encounter it in various situations such as in a book or on TV, they will identify it as a dog. Meanwhile, AI learns to identify a dog by studying a large number of photos tagged as dogs. This process excludes the context that children experience.

Humans also have the imagination to understand new concepts. They can come up

15 with creative ideas and hypotheses, even with limited knowledge. However, AI can only generate novel concepts or solutions based only on its data given by humans, not on its imagination. Without updated information, AI cannot outperform its current knowledge, which consequently limits its ability to innovate in the same way as humans.

Humans also express their ideas and emotions in sophisticated and varied ways

20 through tone, context, and body language, which enhances their interactions. AI lacks real knowledge or emotional experience, even if it can replicate some of these components by learning from data. Thus, AI does not really understand the emotions or meanings behind words, even if it produces human-like text.

UNIT 11    Science and Technology (2)

AI still differs fundamentally from human intelligence, even if it has accomplished amazing achievements in language processing. Personal experience shapes human learning, such as forming creative ideas and expressing emotions in ways that artificial intelligence cannot replicate. This emphasizes the uniqueness of human intelligence and the inability of AI systems to replicate it.

1. Which of the following best describes the key feature of AI and human language processing?
   (A) AI can understand language just like humans do.
   (B) AI only uses existing data, while humans can create new ideas with limited information.
   (C) AI processes information in a similar way to humans.
   (D) The recent improvements of AI show its growing possibilities.

2. According to the passage, which statement is NOT true?
   (A) AI can improve by itself if it gets enough data.
   (B) AI cannot produce the same language as humans because of how it processes information.
   (C) AI's understanding is simpler than that of humans.
   (D) Humans understand new words by connecting them to their real-life experiences.

3. The word "sensory" in line 9 refers to
   (A) Abstract thinking
   (B) Emotional expression
   (C) Information understanding
   (D) Physical perception

4. Why does the author mention how infants acquire the word "dog"?
   (A) To compare AI's learning process with humans'
   (B) To contrast human limitations with AI capabilities
   (C) To emphasize the importance of sensory experiences in interacting with animals
   (D) To show how AI learns through observation

5. The word "replicate" in line 21 is closest in meaning to
   (A) create
   (B) experience
   (C) imitate
   (D) understand

87

6. Which of the following can be inferred from the passage?
   (A) AI is limited by its data and cannot fully understand human language.
   (B) AI will surpass human intelligence in the near future.
   (C) Humans are incapable of learning from AI.
   (D) Humans and AI have the same cognitive processes.

7. The word "This" in line 27 refers to
   (A) The ability of AI to learn through direct experience
   (B) The influence of personal experience on human learning
   (C) The fact that AI has achieved impressive feats in language processing
   (D) The limitations of humans in understanding emotions

8. Which of the following sentences is a paraphrase of the sentence "AI is constrained by the data produced by humans: it cannot create language on its own." in lines 6-7
   (A) AI can produce useful responses, but it cannot generate language without human input.
   (B) AI can generate language from data, but it lacks human creativity.
   (C) AI relies only on the data it has, so it cannot independently create new language.
   (D) Humans can create new ideas, but AI can only work with the data provided by humans.

## Vocabulary Building (Section 3)

> このセクションに登場した単語を辞書で調べ, 意味を書きましょう. また, 調べた単語を使って, 英文を完成させましょう.

(A) consequently　(adv) _____　(D) outperform　(v) _____
(B) constrain　(v) _____　(E) inability　(n) _____
(C) novel　(adj) _____

1. Our company created a _____ design for smartphones.
2. The _____ to connect to the internet stopped the research.
3. This new computer can _____ the older model.

# UNIT 12
# Biology (2)

## 1. Listening Comprehension

Listening Section では問題文は印刷されていないため，用意されている選択肢が事前に内容を推測するための数少ない材料となります．たとえば，Listening Exercises (1) の第1問では，evolution に関連する語がすべての選択肢に出ています．したがって，「進化」に関する何らかの話題が展開されると予想されます．それにとらわれ過ぎることは良くありませんが，前提となる知識枠組みを予め呼び起こすことができれば，聞き取りの負荷が軽くなります．

### Warm up

英語に対応する日本語を選びましょう．

1. balancing    (　)    a. 内部の
2. chemistry    (　)    b. 臓器
3. internal     (　)    c. 化学
4. organ        (　)    d. バランスをとる

### Listening Exercises (1)  2-11, 12

Part B と同じ形式の問題を解きましょう．この Part は，長めの会話とそれに続く複数の質問から成ります．質問に対する最も適切な解答をそれぞれ (A)–(D) から選びましょう．

1. (A) The challenges in teaching evolution to students
   (B) The financial aspects of research in evolutionary biology
   (C) The fascinating aspects of evolutionary change
   (D) The use of technology in modern evolutionary studies

2. (A) The relationship between genetic factors and adaptation
   (B) Drastic changes that happened to life on earth
   (C) Genetically modified animals
   (D) The natural beauty of animals

3. (A) To show some examples of genetic changes
   (B) To remind the student of what she also needs to consider
   (C) To see whether the student remembers what the professor has already taught
   (D) To encourage her not to focus solely on extinct species

## Listening Exercises (2)  2-13, 14

Part C と同じ形式の問題を解きましょう．この Part は，長めの講義・スピーチとそれに続く複数の質問から成ります．質問に対する最も適切な解答をそれぞれ (A)–(D) から選びましょう．

1. (A) The adaptation of organisms to their outside environment
   (B) The maintenance of a stable internal environment in organisms
   (C) A type of cellular reproduction
   (D) The study of human anatomy

2. (A) It helps in changing the genetic makeup.
   (B) It ensures optimal conditions for cell function.
   (C) It increases the organism's size.
   (D) It changes the organism's external appearance.

3. (A) Altering DNA structure
   (B) Regulating body temperature
   (C) Acquiring a new language
   (D) Physical growth over the years

4. (A) A computer running software
   (B) A thermostat regulating temperature
   (C) A plant growing toward light
   (D) A river changing its course

## Vocabulary Building (Section 1)

このセクションに登場した単語を辞書で調べ，意味を書きましょう．また，調べた単語を使って，英文を完成させましょう．

| | | | |
|---|---|---|---|
| (A) steady | (adj) _____ | (D) throw curveballs | (v) _____ |
| (B) uncover | (v) _____ | (E) matter | (v) _____ |
| (C) wonder | (n) _____ | (F) properly | (adv) _____ |

1. Why does homeostasis _____ so much?
2. Homeostasis is all about how living things keep their internal environment _____.
3. If things get too hot, our body's systems can stop working _____.

90

UNIT 12 Biology (2)

## 2. Structure and Written Expression

英語の新聞，雑誌，オンライン記事などを積極的に読み，自然な表現や語法を学びましょう．たくさん読むことで英語の感覚を養っていきましょう．多様なジャンルの文章に触れることで，幅広い知識と表現力も身につけることができます．

### Warm up

英語に対応する日本語を選びましょう．

1. detect        (　)    **a.** 安定した
2. precise       (　)    **b.** 突き止める
3. stable        (　)    **c.** 正確な
4. distinct      (　)    **d.** 個別の

### Structure Exercises

空欄に入る最も適切な語句を (A)–(D) から選び，英文を完成させましょう．

1. The Earth's magnetic field is generated deep within the core at the _____ heart of the planet.

   (A) very
   (B) so
   (C) too
   (D) much

2. In fact, the Earth's magnetic field plays a crucial role in protecting us _____ cosmic rays and other space phenomena.

   (A) from
   (B) away
   (C) off
   (D) aside

3. Humans cannot sense the magnetic field directly, but not a few animals perceive it in various ways _____ navigation and other purposes.

   (A) on
   (B) to
   (C) in
   (D) for

4. The Earth's magnetic field undergoes changes over both short and long _____.

   (A) durations
   (B) circles
   (C) tendencies
   (D) circumstances

91

5. Specialized cells in the eyes of birds have been discovered by researchers, which might _____ them to perceive magnetic fields.

(A) allow
(B) have
(C) make
(D) discourage

6. Similar to the way a magnetic compass helps _____ direction, birds are thought to have a natural "living compass" that allows them to navigate by sensing the Earth's magnetic fields.

(A) in determining
(B) determining
(C) determination
(D) determined

7. Over many years, scientists have dedicated their research to exploring the mechanisms _____ various animals, including birds, sea turtles, fish, and insects, are able to detect and effectively navigate using the magnetic field of the Earth.

(A) in that
(B) by which
(C) for it
(D) where

## Written Expression Exercises

英文中の誤った箇所を (A)–(D) から選びましょう.

1. In the 1830s, Carl Friedrich Gauss <u>found</u> that Earth's main magnetic dipole, which
   <u>A</u>
   comes from <u>inside in</u> the Earth, <u>behaves</u> <u>in a similar way</u>.
   <u>B</u>              <u>C</u>        <u>D</u>

2. While researchers believe <u>further</u> investigation is needed to confirm the precise
   <u>A</u>
   mechanism, they are encouraged by <u>finding</u> that robins , thanks to special molecules, are
   <u>B</u>
   more <u>sensitive for</u> magnetism <u>than</u> non-migratory birds.
   <u>C</u>              <u>D</u>

3. Previous studies have shown that several bird <u>species</u>, <u>especially</u> the European robin
   <u>A</u>      <u>B</u>
   (Erithacus rubecula), <u>relies</u> on Earth's magnetic fields for migration, <u>in addition to</u> visual
   <u>C</u>                                          <u>D</u>
   cues and other signals.

**UNIT 12** Biology (2)

4. The core sources of the stable field, <u>subject to</u> ongoing modifications, often <u>lead</u> to the
                                    **A**                                                **B**
   emergence of short-term shifts or disturbances, <u>that is why</u> momentarily <u>altering</u> the
                                                      **C**                           **D**
   field's usual state.

5. <u>Over the past century,</u> <u>researches on</u> Earth's magnetic field <u>has</u> advanced
             **A**                  **B**                             **C**
   <u>with greater precision.</u>
          **D**

6. <u>To generate</u> a magnetic field via fluid motion, <u>a set of</u> specific conditions <u>must meet</u> to
         **A**                                     **B**                       **C**
   facilitate <u>these processes.</u>
              **D**

7. One can achieve a visualization of the magnetic field <u>by employing</u> a set of
                                                             **A**
   <u>magnetic field lines</u> that are <u>drawn to</u> align with the directional orientation of the field at
             **B**                       **C**
   every <u>distinct points.</u>
             **D**

## *Vocabulary Building* (Section 2)

> このセクションに登場した単語を辞書で調べ，意味を書きましょう．また，調べた単語を使って，
> 英文を完成させましょう．

(A) sensitive    (adj) _____      (D) fluid       (n) _____
(B) distort      (v) _____         (E) facilitate  (v) _____
(C) specialized  (adj) _____      (F) align with  (v) _____

1. Our company's values _____ environmental sustainability.
2. For this kind of mountain climbing, you will need _____ gear that can withstand extreme conditions.
3. It's important to present the facts accurately and not _____ the truth in journalism.

# 3. Reading Comprehension

設問の中には本文の中にヒントとなる単語や表現がはっきり書いていない場合があります．しかしそれでも解答が必ず1つに絞れる根拠があるので筆者の意図や推測することを求める問題でも，基本的に他の問題と解き方は変わりません．

## Warm up

英語に対応する日本語を選びましょう．

1. comprise ( ) **a.** から成る
2. encompassing ( ) **b.** 欠点
3. drawback ( ) **c.** 直面する
4. advocate ( ) **d.** 主張する
5. face ( ) **e.** 網羅的な

## Reading Exercises

次の文章を読み，下の問いに対する最も適切な解答をそれぞれ (A)–(D) から選びましょう．

Adopted by the United Nations in 2015, the Sustainable Development Goals (SDGs) comprise 17 primary objectives to be accomplished by 2030, such as eliminating poverty, offering high-quality education, and addressing climate change. The Millennium Development Goals (MDGs), which were first adopted in 2000 and primarily addressed problems facing

5 developing nations, are where these goals got their start. However, it soon became apparent that many significant areas were left out. The SDGs assumed these objectives and broadened them to include other environmental, social, and economic considerations.

Numerous nations and groups participated in lengthy consultations during the SDGs' development process. The process started with a decision made during the 2012 Rio+20

10 United Nations Conference on Sustainable Development. This was a part of the global effort to find a more all-encompassing and common solution to global issues. Subsequently, the SDGs have directed global endeavors to attain economic, social, and environmental sustainability, grounded in the concept of "leaving no one behind." Many nations and organizations are attempting to adopt the SDGs because of their attention-grabbing

15 development and implementation as a new paradigm for global collaboration. They are endeavoring to integrate these objectives into their domestic policies.

The fact that the SDGs offer a shared framework for the global community to work toward sustainable development is one of their advantages. As a result, nations can work together to accomplish the goals, and rules for allocating funds and setting policy priorities are

20 provided. By considering all sectors of the economy, society, and environment, the SDGs also advocate for a holistic strategy to promote sustainable development. But there are drawbacks as well. The complexity and number of the goals might make it challenging to create implementation strategies that are unique to the circumstances of each nation. Concerns have

also been raised about the possibility that the difficulties in obtaining funds and setting up a reliable monitoring system may cause the aims' advancement to be delayed. Nevertheless, the SDGs represent a significant advancement in bringing attention to and promoting action on the numerous urgent global concerns.

1. What are the SDGs?
   (A) A series of recommendations for improving education in developing countries
   (B) A set of objectives established by the United Nations to achieve a sustainable future
   (C) A list of global challenges identified by the Rio+20 conference
   (D) A range of financial assistance programs for developing nations

2. What previous initiative were the development of the SDGs based on?
   (A) The 2012 Rio+20 United Nations Conference on Sustainable Development
   (B) The World Health Organization's health targets
   (C) The Millennium Development Goals (MDGs)
   (D) The United Nations Security Council resolutions

3. What is the main reason the SDGs were created?
   (A) To replace the MDGs with a more comprehensive set of goals
   (B) To address environmental issues neglected by the United Nations
   (C) To provide financial assistance to developing countries
   (D) To establish a new United Nations conference on sustainability

4. According to the passage, how were the SDGs developed?
   (A) Through a rapid decision made by the UN Security Council
   (B) By discussion with a small group of environmental experts
   (C) Following extensive consultations with various stakeholders
   (D) Based on research conducted by a single UN agency

5. What is the concept of "leaving no one behind" in the context of the SDGs?
   (A) Ensuring all UN member states contribute equally to achieving the goals
   (B) Focusing on helping those who are most in need of support
   (C) Prioritizing economic growth over environmental sustainability
   (D) Encouraging competition between nations in achieving the goals

6. What is an advantage of the SDGs?
   (A) They provide a clear timeline for achieving specific goals.
   (B) They offer a framework for international cooperation on sustainability.
   (C) They focus solely on environmental issues.
   (D) They are easily adaptable to each country's unique situation.

7. What is a potential challenge for implementing the SDGs?

(A) Lack of public awareness about the goals

(B) Difficulty in measuring progress towards the goals

(C) Limited participation from developed nations

(D) The large number and complexity of the goals

8. What is the main idea of the passage?

(A) The SDGs are a perfect solution to all the world's problems.

(B) The SDGs are a comprehensive and ambitious plan to achieve a sustainable future for all.

(C) The SDGs are a new set of goals that will replace the MDGs.

(D) The SDGs are a traditional and challenging project, but they represent a significant step forward in addressing global problems.

## Vocabulary Building (Section 3)

> このセクションに登場した単語を辞書で調べ，意味を書きましょう．また，調べた単語を使って，英文を完成させましょう．

(A) eliminate　(v) _____　　(D) attention-grabbing　(adj) _____

(B) assume　(v) _____　　(E) holistic　(adj) _____

(C) endeavor　(n) _____

1. A(n) _____ to solve the complex problem was undertaken by the research team.

2. The new product design features a(n) _____ color scheme.

3. Our team worked hard to _____ all errors in the software code.

# UNIT 13

# Art (2)

## 1. Listening Comprehension

専門用語と並んで，固有名詞についても聞き取りが難しいものの一つです．特に，日本語の中にカタカナで入ってきている人名などは，事前に知っている人物であっても認識できない場合もあるので注意が必要です．正確にスペルを書ける必要はないので，人物であれば，何をしたと述べられているか，他の人物との共通点や関係性にはどのような言及があるのかなど，可能な範囲でメモをとっていきましょう．

### Warm up

英語に対応する日本語を選びましょう．

1. prototype     (　)     a. 原型
2. bebop         (　)     b. 作曲家
3. genre         (　)     c. ビバップ
4. composer      (　)     d. 様式・形式

### Listening Exercises (1)     2-15〜17

Part A と同じ形式の問題を解きましょう．この Part は，短い会話とそれに続く1つの質問から成ります．質問に対する最も適切な解答をそれぞれ (A)–(D) から選びましょう．

1. (A) The abstract techniques and use of vibrant colors
   (B) His use of light and shadow and depiction of emotion
   (C) The focus on landscape and nature in his works
   (D) The geometric patterns and modernist approach in his paintings

2. (A) The historical background of jazz music
   (B) The cost and location of the concert
   (C) Live improvisation and musician interaction
   (D) The different types of jazz music genres

3. (A) The technical aspects of opera performance
   (B) The transition of opera from classic to modern
   (C) Biographies of contemporary opera singers
   (D) Opera's influence on modern music genres

97

## Listening Exercises (2)  CD 2-18, 19

Part C と同じ形式の問題を解きましょう．この Part は，長めの講義・スピーチとそれに続く複数の質問から成ります．質問に対する最も適切な解答をそれぞれ (A)–(D) から選びましょう．

1. (A) The life of Louis Armstrong
   (B) The evolution of jazz
   (C) The music of African Americans
   (D) The city of New Orleans

2. (A) New York
   (B) Chicago
   (C) New Orleans
   (D) Los Angeles

3. (A) Duke Ellington
   (B) Jelly Roll Morton
   (C) Neil Alden Armstrong
   (D) Ewa Aulin

4. (A) It focuses on improvisation.
   (B) It has a bouncy rhythm.
   (C) It originated in New Orleans.
   (D) It was popularized by Louis Armstrong.

## Vocabulary Building (Section 1)

このセクションに登場した単語を辞書で調べ，意味を書きましょう．また，調べた単語を使って，英文を完成させましょう．

| | | | | | |
|---|---|---|---|---|---|
| (A) notable | (adj) _____ | | (D) improvisation | (n) _____ | |
| (B) resonate | (v) _____ | | (E) originate | (v) _____ | |
| (C) multitude | (n) _____ | | (F) bouncy | (adj) _____ | |

1. Jazz has spread to various regions around the world, creating a(n) _____ of styles.
2. Various factors enabled Jazz to _____ in African American communities in the late 19th to early 20th century.
3. The _____ and energy of live jazz is incredible.

98

UNIT 13 | Art (2)

## 2. Structure and Written Expression

自然な英語表現の知識は重要です．よく使われる単語の組み合わせ（コロケーション）を学ぶことで，文法・語法問題の正答率が上がります．例えば，make a decision や play a crutial role などの組み合わせを覚えることです．コロケーションの知識はあらゆる面で役に立ちます．

### Warm up

英語に対応する日本語を選びましょう．

1. pivotal （　）　　**a.** 主要な
2. heritage （　）　　**b.** 有名な
3. renowned （　）　　**c.** 遺産
4. captivating （　）　　**d.** 魅力的な

### Structure Exercises

空欄に入る最も適切な語句を (A)–(D) から選び，英文を完成させましょう．

1. The piano style known as ragtime, characterized by its unique syncopated rhythms, represented a new musical genre that played a key role _____ the emergence of jazz music.

    (A) to signal
    (B) signal
    (C) in signaling
    (D) on signaling

2. A new musical approach _____ M-Base emerged, which integrated the traditions of jazz and funk music.

    (A) called
    (B) to call
    (C) calling
    (D) calls

3. A blend of various cultural and musical heritages, _____ initially called "jass" was born within the African American community and was quickly embraced by musicians from diverse backgrounds.

    (A) that
    (B) the music
    (C) it
    (D) which

4. Jazz faced criticism for being "in poor taste", much like rock 'n' roll and hip-hop would later, often by _____ who were unfamiliar with the music.

    (A) those
    (B) them
    (C) these
    (D) they

99

5. Early jazz emerged from a fusion of the relaxed style of blues and the rhythms of ragtime, _____ enriched by diverse historical influences.

(A) following
(B) previous
(C) further
(D) original

6. Jazz music boasts vast diversity; _____, it typically features a rhythmic swing, along with the distinct use of bent or blue notes.

(A) although
(B) despite
(C) contrary
(D) however

7. In its formative years, jazz saw the rise of specific styles such as swing and big band, _____ icons like Louis Armstrong and Fletcher Henderson playing significant roles in shaping its history.

(A) on
(B) with
(C) in
(D) to

## Written Expression Exercises

英文中の誤った箇所を (A)–(D) から選びましょう.

1. Afro-Cuban jazz combines the <u>detailed</u> rhythms of <u>traditionally</u> Afro-Cuban music with
                                   **A**                      **B**
   the <u>smooth</u> harmonies and <u>spontaneous</u> creativity of American jazz.
       **C**                **D**

2. Jazz musicians once struggled <u>to</u> recognition, <u>but</u> today they are widely <u>celebrated for</u>
                                **A**         **B**               **C**
   their artistic innovation and <u>influence on</u> various music genres.
                         **D**

3. The <u>uniqueness</u> of each jazz performance comes from the <u>distinct</u> styles of the players
       **A**                                   **B**
   and their impromptu solos, which <u>serves</u> to transform a familiar tune into an <u>entirely</u> new
                               **C**                          **D**
   creation.

4. Ragtime, <u>a musical form</u> with African American roots, <u>stands for</u> its emphasis on
           **A**                           **B**
   syncopation and emerged from the skills of <u>renowned</u> pianists in the Mississippi and
                                       **C**
   Missouri river areas <u>during</u> the late 19th century.
                    **D**

**UNIT 13** Art (2)

5. Jazz, <u>came out</u> in the early 1900s in the United States, <u>particularly</u> flourished in New
   <br>　　　　A　　　　　　　　　　　　　　　　　　　　　　B
   Orleans, <u>where</u> its diverse population of African, French, Caribbean, and <u>other</u> heritages
   <br>　　　　C　　　　　　　　　　　　　　　　　　　　　　　　　　　　　D
   played a pivotal role in its development.

6. New Orleans, <u>known for</u> its liberal culture, <u>featuring</u> vibrant music and rich
   <br>　　　　　　　A　　　　　　　　　　　　B
   <u>culinary traditions</u>, <u>and attracts</u> visitors seeking a unique cultural experience.
   <br>　　C　　　　　　　　　D

7. Regina Carter, who was born in Detroit in 1966 and <u>initially</u> began as a classical
   <br>　　　　　　　　　　　　　　　　　　　　　　　　　　　　A
   violinist, made a significant shift <u>to her career</u>, <u>motivated by</u> the captivating and free-
   <br>　　　　　　　　　　　　　　　　B　　　　　　　C
   spirited performances <u>of</u> French jazz violinist Stéphane Grappelli.
   <br>　　　　　　　　　　　D

## 🎧 *Vocabulary Building* (Section 2)

> このセクションに登場した単語を辞書で調べ, 意味を書きましょう. また, 調べた単語を使って, 英文を完成させましょう.

(A) fusion　　(n) ＿＿＿＿＿＿＿　　　　(D) formative　(adj) ＿＿＿＿＿＿＿

(B) criticism　(n) ＿＿＿＿＿＿＿　　　　(E) celebrate　(v) ＿＿＿＿＿＿＿

(C) diverse　(adj) ＿＿＿＿＿＿＿　　　　(F) flourish　(v) ＿＿＿＿＿＿＿

1. Many people ＿＿＿＿＿ Mahatma Gandhi for his nonviolent approach to achieving political and social change.

2. The years spent studying abroad were ＿＿＿＿＿ for her, shaping her worldview and influencing her future career path.

3. After the long rainy season, the garden started to ＿＿＿＿＿, with flowers blooming in bright and lively colors everywhere.

101

# 3. Reading Comprehension

実際の ITP テストでは 1 つのパッセージに 10 個の問題がついています．5 つのパッセージがありますから 55 分で 50 問，つまり 1 問 1 分で問題を解く必要があります．時間のかかるものとそうでないものがありますが，質問文のパターンからある程度予想できます．

## Warm up

英語に対応する日本語を選びましょう．

1. amalgamation （　）　　**a.** 献身
2. pinnacle （　）　　**b.** 多才さ
3. introspection （　）　　**c.** 頂点
4. versatility （　）　　**d.** 内省
5. commitment （　）　　**e.** 融合

## Reading Exercises

次の文章を読み，下の問いに対する最も適切な解答をそれぞれ (A)–(D) から選びましょう．

The jazz genre, which has strong historical and cultural ties to New Orleans, represents the quintessential example of the American music culture. The origin of this phenomenon can be attributed to the distinctive nature of the urban environment, which is characterized by a dynamic amalgamation of musical customs originating from the African American, French,
5　Spanish, and British populations that gathered in the city during the 19th century. The combination of these elements facilitated the emergence of a unique blend of auditory elements, enhanced by the significant impact of African American spirituals and labor songs, which subsequently served as the bedrock of jazz.

　　Jazz evolved over time to mirror the shifting dynamics of American society. The
10　period known as the "swing" era, spanning from the 1920s to the 1940s, was widely regarded as the pinnacle of jazz. Swing music, distinguished by its captivating rhythms and wide-ranging appeal to audiences, emerged as a fundamental element of American entertainment, with renowned individuals like Louis Armstrong and Duke Ellington leading this artistic movement. During the 1940s and 1950s, the genre underwent a shift towards introspection
15　with the emergence of bebop. Bebop, characterized by its complex melodies, rapid tempos, and emphasis on improvisation, propelled jazz towards a trajectory that valued individual virtuosity and a concentration on the musicians themselves.

　　Contemporary jazz demonstrates its versatility by integrating components from various genres, including Latin, funk, and even hip-hop. The continuous innovation
20　emphasizes the exceptional adaptability of jazz. Improvisation is a fundamental aspect of jazz's identity, serving as a defining feature that enables musicians to generate music in a spontaneous manner. This methodology provides audiences with distinctive encounters that show both ingenuity and technical expertise, setting jazz apart from classical music and

102

reinforcing its fundamental principles of liberty and self-expression.

The influence of jazz transcends its geographical origins, exerting a lasting impact on    25
various musical genres including rock, pop, and soul. Numerous artists from various musical
genres attest to its lasting impact. Jazz, as a dynamic and continuously evolving art form,
serves as a source of inspiration and a means of expressing the richness of the human
experience, owing to its extensive historical background and constant commitment to
innovation.    30

1. What is the main purpose of the passage?
   (A) To explain the influence of New Orleans on jazz
   (B) To describe the evolution and characteristics of jazz
   (C) To compare jazz with other musical genres
   (D) To argue for the superiority of jazz over classical music

2. What contributed to the emergence of jazz in New Orleans?
   (A) The city's economic prosperity
   (B) A blend of diverse musical traditions
   (C) The invention of new musical instruments
   (D) Government support for the arts

3. The word "quintessential" in line 2 is closest in meaning to
   (A) unique
   (B) original
   (C) typical
   (D) basic

4. According to the third paragraph, what is special about jazz music?
   (A) Musicians can make up music as they perform.
   (B) Jazz is difficult to play because of improvisation.
   (C) The core of jazz music is planned performances.
   (D) Making music on the spot is not important in jazz.

5. Why are Louis Armstrong and Duke Ellington mentioned?
   (A) They started jazz.
   (B) They helped make jazz popular.
   (C) They were important musicians in the swing era.
   (D) They showed that jazz has many different styles.

6. The word "transcends" in line 25 is closest in meaning to
   (A) moves beyond
   (B) decreases
   (C) changes
   (D) complicates


7. What is important about improvisation in jazz?
   (A) It started with bebop music.
   (B) It is not as important now as before.
   (C) It makes jazz different from other kinds of music.
   (D) It caused disagreements among jazz musicians early on.


8. It can be inferred from the passage that jazz music
   (A) has remained unchanged since its inception.
   (B) is considered more important than classical music.
   (C) encourages creative freedom and expression.
   (D) is losing popularity due to its complexity.

## *Vocabulary Building* (Section 3)

> このセクションに登場した単語を辞書で調べ, 意味を書きましょう. また, 調べた単語を使って, 英文を完成させましょう.

(A) emergence   (n) _____     (D) attribute   (v) _____
(B) bedrock     (n) _____     (E) expertise   (n) _____
(C) spearhead   (v) _____

1. A group of young artists is _____ing a new art movement.
2. The art historian shared her _____ on the painting with the audience.
3. The _____ of the electric guitar greatly changed popular music.

# UNIT 14

# Economics (2)

## 1. Listening Comprehension

最後の Unit は経済学です．Part C は 1 名の話者によるまとまりのある発話から成るため，Reading Section と同様に論理的に理解することも重要です．代表的なものとして，列挙，分類，比較，対比，順序，因果関係などの構造をおさえておきましょう．また，段落が目に見えないため，話題の転換は，聞き取った語やイントネーションから見極める必要があります．談話標識 (first, second, in addition, moreover, on the other hand など) にも注目してみてください．

### Warm up

英語に対応する日本語を選びましょう．

1. thrive       (  )    a. 要旨
2. groundwork   (  )    b. 知識をもった
3. gist         (  )    c. 基礎
4. savvy        (  )    d. 繁栄する

### Listening Exercises (1)   2-20〜22

Part A と同じ形式の問題を解きましょう．この Part は，短い会話とそれに続く 1 つの質問から成ります．質問に対する最も適切な解答をそれぞれ (A)–(D) から選びましょう．

1. (A) The negative aspects of their functionality
   (B) The limitations of smartphones in daily life
   (C) The convenience that smartphones offer
   (D) The problem of information overload

2. (A) The efficient application of artificial intelligence
   (B) The impact of global warming on wildlife
   (C) An effective way of brainstorming
   (D) Progress in medical technology

3. (A) Transportation systems
   (B) The history of steam engines
   (C) The mechanics of steam engines
   (D) Modern applications of steam engines

105

### Listening Exercises (2)    2-23, 24

Part C と同じ形式の問題を解きましょう．この Part は，長めの講義・スピーチとそれに続く複数の質問から成ります．質問に対する最も適切な解答をそれぞれ (A)–(D) から選びましょう．

1. (A) Learning only about financial accounting
   (B) Understanding how to run a business effectively
   (C) Focusing solely on marketing strategies
   (D) Studying the history of commerce

2. (A) It focuses specifically on one industry.
   (B) The skills learned are exclusively applicable to technology fields.
   (C) The skills learned can be applied in various industries.
   (D) It is almost entirely about learning theoretical concepts.

3. (A) Only human resource management
   (B) Only how to start a new business
   (C) Management, financial, marketing, and human resources principles
   (D) Just the legal aspects of running a business

4. (A) Only technical skills
   (B) Strategic thinking and leadership
   (C) Just artistic skills
   (D) Solely computer programming skills

### Vocabulary Building (Section 1)

> このセクションに登場した単語を辞書で調べ，意味を書きましょう．また，調べた単語を使って，英文を完成させましょう．

(A) master    (v) _____    (D) agile    (adj) _____
(B) versatile (adj) _____    (E) eye    (v) _____
(C) prep     (v) _____    (F) map out (v) _____

1. Smart phones are among the most _____ inventions because they can perform a variety of tasks.

2. To start her own business, she wanted to _____ the art of managing every aspect of a company.

3. As you _____ your academic journey, you might want to give Business Administration a thought!

106

UNIT 14 Economics (2)

## 2. Structure and Written Expression

英語の基本文型を理解しましょう. 主語 - 動詞一致の問題では, 基本的な英語の文型 (SV, SVO 等 ) を理解しておく必要があります. 主語と動詞の位置関係を把握し, 正しい文法関係を見抜くことができるようになりましょう. その際, 例外的な文法事項にも注意してください.

### Warm up

英語に対応する日本語を選びましょう.

1. medieval      (   )     **a.** 規律
2. substantial      (   )     **b.** 大規模な
3. inhabitant      (   )     **c.** 住人
4. discipline      (   )     **d.** 中世の

### Structure Exercises

空欄に入る最も適切な語句を (A)–(D) から選び, 英文を完成させましょう.

1. Paper money, which made its first appearance in Western societies in the 17th century, ＿＿＿ a substantial shift in economic practices.

   (A) marked
   (B) obliged
   (C) accommodated
   (D) confused

2. During the time when lords controlled land, people paid for its use with labor and crops, but the shift to a money-based system ＿＿＿ different social systems.

   (A) led to
   (B) caused by
   (C) resulting in
   (D) helping

3. The revival of a money economy in medieval Europe was a ＿＿＿ shift in the nature of feudal society.

   (A) retrospective
   (B) irrespective
   (C) respectful
   (D) fundamental

4. One of the first types of money was natural ＿＿＿, like cowrie shells, which people used as currency in ancient times.

   (A) artifacts
   (B) matters
   (C) environments
   (D) objects

107

5. The Great Depression, spanning from 1929 to roughly 1939, led countries to reevaluate the gold standard, and by the 1970s, _____ resulted in the separation of gold from their currencies.

(A) which
(B) this
(C) one
(D) these

6. Although the concept of credit is age-old, the first universal credit card didn't make its debut _____ 1950.

(A) through
(B) until
(C) later
(D) by

7. In his work *Living Currency*, Klossowski explored the process _____ human qualities in an economic society.

(A) to lose
(B) of losing
(C) for losing
(D) on losing

### Written Expression Exercises

英文中の誤った箇所を (A)–(D) から選びましょう.

1. Whale teeth were <u>other</u> form of natural currency <u>used by</u> Fijians, while the inhabitants of
        **A**                      **B**
   Yap Island, now a part of Micronesia, used limestone discs, <u>which</u> evolved into a form of
                                              **C**
   money still <u>recognized</u> in their culture today.
            **D**

2. As money <u>reflected</u> the characteristics of social cohesion and the nature of public
          **A**
   authority, European society <u>needed</u> coins that intimidatingly <u>displays</u> strict discipline and
                   **B**                      **C**
   the <u>ruler's</u> authority.
      **D**

3. While Sweden <u>was expanding</u> into the Baltic region, it had <u>limiting</u> access to silver and
              **A**                        **B**
   gold, so the new Era of Great Power required <u>a substantial amount of</u> silver coins
                                          **C**
   <u>to sustain</u> its mercenary armies and maintain its advantage.
     **D**

4. In the period <u>where</u> parchment was the <u>primary</u> material for books, paper money <u>was not</u>
             **A**                   **B**                     **C**
   yet come into use in <u>the Western world</u>.
               **D**

UNIT 14 Economics (2)

5. About the 6th century BCE, animal hides <u>were being transformed</u> into currency, <u>method</u>
   <u>   </u>**A**                 **B**          **C**
that was reportedly in use in <u>early</u> ancient Rome.
               **D**

6. When paper money <u>was introduced</u> in China in the 13th century, it was <u>made from</u>
              **A**                   **B**
mulberry tree wood, and guards were stationed around the forests to <u>protect</u>, with
                                 **C**
counterfeiters <u>facing</u> death as punishment.
        **D**

7. Paper, <u>believed to be</u> invented in China, <u>led to</u> the introduction of paper currency <u>during</u>
       **A**                **B**                  **C**
Emperor Zhenzong's reign <u>between</u> 997 and 1022 CE.
                **D**

## 🦇 *Vocabulary Building* (Section 2)

> このセクションに登場した単語を辞書で調べ, 意味を書きましょう. また, 調べた単語を使って,
> 英文を完成させましょう.

(A) currency    (n) _____    (D) reign    (n) _____
(B) intimidatingly    (adv) _____    (E) reportedly    (adv) _____
(C) counterfeit    (adj) _____    (F) feudal    (adj) _____

1. The police discovered _____ bills circulating in the city's markets.
2. During her 20-year _____, the queen introduced reforms that transformed the kingdom's social environment.
3. The famous actor, _____ cast in a major role for the upcoming film, was spotted at a popular café yesterday.

109

# 3. Reading Comprehension

Reading Section は，最後のセクションである同時に，もっとも時間がかかる，かつ設問数も多い箇所です．時間が足りなくなるととりあえずマークだけしておく，という場合もあるかもしれませんが，短時間で解答できる問題（語彙，指示）もあるので最後まであきらめないようにしましょう．

## Warm up

英語に対応する日本語を選びましょう．

| | | | | | |
|---|---|---|---|---|---|
| **1.** pseudonym | ( ) | | **a.** 徹底的な |
| **2.** decentralized | ( ) | | **b.** 偽名 |
| **3.** apprehension | ( ) | | **c.** 耐久性・耐久力 |
| **4.** thorough | ( ) | | **d.** 不安・心配 |
| **5.** durability | ( ) | | **e.** 分散的な |

## Reading Exercises

次の文章を読み，下の問いに対する最も適切な解答をそれぞれ (A)–(D) から選びましょう．

Cryptocurrency, a type of digital currency, has a long history that covers multiple decades. Its origin can be traced back to visionaries who aimed to create safe Internet payment systems. In the 1980s, Dutch researcher David Chaum established the concept, emphasizing privacy and trust. He devised a method for securely exchanging digital tokens without relying
5 on a central authority. Chaum's eCash, though short-lived, established the foundation for upcoming advancements. In 2008, an individual or collective using the pseudonym Satoshi Nakamoto presented a paper that revolutionized the financial sector by introducing Bitcoin. Bitcoin implemented a decentralized system that minimized dependence on central banks and utilized blockchain technology to ensure the security of transactions.

10 Utilizing cryptocurrency presents advantages as well as obstacles. One advantage is the independence from central banks, which can lead to increased financial autonomy. Transactions are secure because of blockchain technology, which inhibits fraud. It is accessible to anyone with Internet connectivity regardless of their location.

Nevertheless, issues persist. Cryptocurrencies can experience significant fluctuations
15 in value, and cause concern. Ambiguous regulations hinder the adoption of the system by a larger number of individuals. Certain cryptocurrencies utilize a mechanism called proof-of-work to validate transactions, which consumes significant amounts of energy and creates environmental apprehensions. Users lack protection due to the absence of insurance for the funds they invest in Bitcoin exchanges.

20 The future of Bitcoin is promising, although there are obstacles that need to be addressed. There has been a remarkable shift from Chaum's eCash to the development of Bitcoin. Whether it achieves global currency status or remains a specialist asset, its influence

is evident. As the popularity of cryptocurrency increases, it is essential to have a thorough understanding of it. Knowing what digital currency might mean for our financial future is crucial, as the world changes. Advancements in technology will enhance system efficiency and reliability. Emerging technologies such as hydrogen fuel cells and wave energy capture devices demonstrate significant potential.

The evolution of cryptocurrency, from its initial trials to its widespread adoption, mirrors our pursuit of economic independence and durability. Its impact will persist in shaping our transaction methods, investments, and perspective on our digital future.

1. The passage mainly discusses
   (A) the history and future of online payment systems
   (B) the technical details of how cryptocurrency works
   (C) the advantages and disadvantages of cryptocurrency
   (D) the life and work of David Chaum

2. Who is credited with laying the foundation for future advancements in cryptocurrency?
   (A) Satoshi Nakamoto
   (B) David Chaum
   (C) A Dutch researcher
   (D) Visionaries of the 1980s

3. The word "established" in line 3 is closest in meaning to
   (A) proposed
   (B) banned
   (C) explained
   (D) ignored

4. What is the author's main purpose in writing this passage?
   (A) To persuade readers to invest in cryptocurrency
   (B) To explain the technical workings of blockchain technology
   (C) To provide an overview of cryptocurrency and its prospects
   (D) To criticize the environmental impact of cryptocurrency

5. The word "It" in line 12 refers to
   (A) Cryptocurrency
   (B) The Internet
   (C) Blockchain technology
   (D) Financial autonomy

**6.** What is the main point of the third paragraph?
(A) To describe the benefits of cryptocurrency
(B) To explain the security features of Bitcoin
(C) To highlight the challenges of cryptocurrency
(D) To compare different types of digital currencies

**7.** What is one potential environmental concern associated with certain cryptocurrencies?
(A) Overuse of metal
(B) Harmful emission of electric waves
(C) Disposal of currently used bills
(D) Excessive energy consumption

**8.** How does the author feel about the future of cryptocurrency?
(A) Optimistic and hopeful
(B) Skeptical and doubtful
(C) Neutral and objective
(D) Angry and frustrated

## Vocabulary Building (Section 3)

このセクションに登場した単語を辞書で調べ, 意味を書きましょう. また, 調べた単語を使って, 英文を完成させましょう.

(A) visionary    (n) _____    (D) inhibit    (v) _____
(B) transaction    (n) _____    (E) persist    (v) _____
(C) autonomy    (n) _____

**1.** A(n) _____ can create new markets and grow their company.
**2.** Businesses can foster employee creativity by respecting their _____.
**3.** Regulations can _____ economic growth.

## TEXT PRODUCTION STAFF

| edited by | 編集 |
|---|---|
| Eiichi Tamura | 田村 栄一 |
| Fumi Matsumoto | 松本 風見 |

| cover design by | 表紙デザイン |
|---|---|
| Nobuyoshi Fujino | 藤野 伸芳 |

| DTP by | DTP |
|---|---|
| ALIUS (Hiroyuki Kinouchi) | アリウス（木野内 宏行） |

## CD PRODUCTION STAFF

| recorded by | 吹き込み者 |
|---|---|
| Vinay Murthy (AmE) | ヴィナイ・ムルティ（アメリカ英語） |
| Jack Merluzzi (AmE) | ジャック・マルージ（アメリカ英語） |
| Jennifer Okano (AmE) | ジェニファー・オカノ（アメリカ英語） |

## TOPIC-FOCUSED APPROACH TO THE TOEFL ITP® TEST
### 頻出トピックで攻略するTOEFL ITP® TEST 実践演習

2025年1月20日　初版発行
2025年2月15日　第2刷発行

著　　者　小倉 雅明　青田 庄真　関谷 弘毅
　　　　　Arnold Arao　鬼頭 和也　佐藤 健

発 行 者　佐野 英一郎

発 行 所　株式会社 成美堂
　　　　　〒101-0052　東京都千代田区神田小川町3-22
　　　　　TEL 03-3291-2261　FAX 03-3293-5490
　　　　　https://www.seibido.co.jp

印 刷・製 本　倉敷印刷株式会社

ISBN 978-4-7919-7315-6　　　　　　　　　　　　　Printed in Japan

・落丁・乱丁本はお取り替えします。
・本書の無断複写は、著作権上の例外を除き著作権侵害となります。